Survey Basics

Patricia Pulliam Phillips, Jack J. Phillips,
and Bruce Aaron

ASTD
PRESS

Alexandria, Virginia

ASTD Press is an internationally renowned source of insightful and practical information on workplace learning, performance, and professional development.

ASTD Press
1640 King Street Box 1443
Alexandria, VA 22313-1443 USA

Ordering information: Books published by ASTD Press can be purchased by visiting ASTD's website at store.astd.org or by calling 800.628.2783 or 703.683.8100.

Library of Congress Control Number: 2012955500

ISBN-10: 1-56286-809-8
ISNB-13: 978-1-56286-809-3
e-ISBN: 978-1-60728-783-4

ASTD Press Editorial Staff:
Director: Glenn Saltzman
Editor and Manager, ASTD Press: Ashley McDonald
Community of Practice Manager, Learning and Development: Juana Llorens
Editorial Assistant: Sarah Cough
Cover Design: Lon Levy
Text Design: Marisa Kelly

Printed by Victor Graphics, Inc., Baltimore, MD, www.victorgraphics.com

Contents

Preface

▪ ▪

General Description

"Can you help us with survey design?" This question is routinely asked at the end of our measurement and evaluation and ROI workshops. Learning and development professionals worldwide have embraced the concept of measurement, evaluation, and ROI. They know the importance of collecting valid, reliable data. But many want to build greater skill in asking the right measurement questions the right way.

Survey design and administration are paramount to collecting data useful to decision makers. Whether conducting a comprehensive needs assessment or evaluating a learning event, data needs lead to the use of surveys and questionnaires. *Survey Basics* is a tool to help the learning and development professional design and administer surveys and questionnaires. It describes the purpose of surveys and questionnaires, types of errors that can creep into survey results, and considerations when developing specific survey questions. In addition, it offers tips and tricks to ensure a positive response rate as well as techniques useful in designing the instrument so that individuals find it easy to respond. The book includes content on research design, data summary and reporting, and a variety of examples of different types of survey questions and instruments.

In addition to content on survey design, the book includes information on survey technologies and provides a process readers can use to make decisions about which is the best technology for them. By applying this simple decision-making process, readers can identify the most appropriate survey tool for their needs.

After reading this book, readers will be able to:

1. Avoid potential errors found in surveys.
2. Develop SMART survey objectives.
3. Develop appropriate survey questions, given the survey's purpose and objectives.
4. Identify weaknesses in survey questions by comparing well-written and poorly written questions.
5. Identify the target respondents to whom the survey is administered.
6. Identify survey technologies that support development and administration of surveys.
7. Report data so that they are perceived as usable and relevant to the target audience.

By reading the text and completing exercises, readers will be able to develop a survey or questionnaire that captures valid, reliable, and usable data. Action steps will guide readers through the actual development of a questionnaire for a program or project important to them. Using the Evaluation/ROI blog made available through ASTD, readers will receive additional support on the development of their survey instruments.

Authored by the co-founders of the ROI Institute along with a former executive at Accenture with global responsibilities for training, evaluation, and knowledge sharing, the book provides readers with a practical guide to develop surveys and questionnaires, with a particular focus on self-administered questionnaires. While the book offers basic instruction on survey design, resources are made available in the back of the book for those readers who want to learn even more.

Need for the Book

The learning and development community's interest in designing surveys and questionnaires has never been greater than it is today. With the growth of measurement and evaluation practices, the focus on capturing performance data, and the renewal of the needs assessment, developing practical, yet valid, surveys and questionnaires is fundamental to most learning and development functions. Yet, there are no books that provide a practical framework for developing these tools that target the learning and development professional.

There are many books on survey and questionnaire design. Some of the well-known titles include:

Fink, A. (2002). *Survey Toolkit,* 2nd **edition. Thousand Oaks: Sage Publications.** This series of books provides a practical tool for researchers interested in designing and administering surveys, interviews, and focus groups. In addition, the kit includes a book on reporting results and data analysis. While the tool is useful and one of the more practical series on the market, it does target the social science researcher rather than the learning and development professional.

Rea, L.M., and Parker, R.A. (2005). *Designing and Conducting Survey Research: A Comprehensive Guide.* **San Francisco: Jossey-Bass.** Another comprehensive guide to designing survey research, this text is just that—a full board textbook. Useful to researchers, particularly those pursuing doctoral theses and dissertations, the book provides a complete perspective of survey research design. However, the book does not target the learning and development professional and is much greater in scope than *Survey Basics.*

Fowler, F.J. (2008). *Survey Research Methods,* 4th **edition. Thousand Oaks: Sage Publications.** This book is an excellent text on survey design. It covers many of the same issues covered in other survey design books plus offers discussion on the expanding use of mobile phones as a potential data gathering tool. It targets academic readers and social researchers, but again, lacks a focus on business research.

Dillman, D.A., Smyth, J.D., and Christian, L.M. (2009). *Internet, Mail, and Mixed-Mode Surveys: The Tailored Design Method.* **San Francisco: John Wiley.** A classic text used in academia, this book has helped many doctoral students survive their survey research. All 512 pages make this book one of the most comprehensive texts on survey design. Dillman, et al. provide five steps to ensure a successful response on survey administration and offer comprehensive research that supports this process. This book is a must for any student of survey design.

These texts are just a few of the excellent survey design books available on the market today. They serve as references for *Survey Basics* content. But they miss the key ingredients needed for the recipe to support the learning professional:

- ▶ exercises for reflective learning
- ▶ tools for planning and implementing surveys in the learning and development practice
- ▶ reference to issues learning and development professionals face on a routine basis
- ▶ survey samples offered by learning professionals for learning professionals
- ▶ action steps to guide readers as they develop a survey or questionnaire
- ▶ the ASTD brand.

Audience

The primary audience for this book is the learning and development professional who must design surveys and questionnaires to collect data for the purpose of conducting needs assessments and evaluating program results. As one of the authors has repeatedly witnessed during measurement and evaluation workshops, learning and development professionals are calling for help in developing good data collection instruments. Informal surveys of workshop participants show that the majority of participants want a course on survey design and administration. This book will supplement any course offered to this important target audience.

A second audience is managers of learning and development professionals. Managers do not need to be experts in survey design, but they need to know enough to help coach their team and be proactive in the data collection process. This book is perfect for the learning and development manager in that it gives just enough information to develop solid surveys without the enormous undertaking of reading an academic text.

A third audience is faculty of human resource development, learning and development, and human performance technology academic programs. These programs offer at least one course that includes a focus on survey design and administration. Most of these programs target the scholar-practitioner, requiring less technical expertise in research and more research-based tools designed for application. The book is perfect for that type of course. Also, graduate students pursuing their thesis and dissertation research will appreciate this book as it provides the basic elements with which they need to be concerned in planning their research projects.

A fourth target audience includes meetings and events professionals. The meetings and events industry is closely aligned with the learning and development industry. In some cases, organizations place meetings and events professionals within the learning and development function. For example, in one recent ROI workshop held for Meetings Professionals International (MPI), two participants who were meetings and events professionals made a point of noting that they report to the learning and development function. During the 2011 COCAL conference in Viña del Mar, Chile, 17 March 2011, one participant asked specifically, "Do you have a resource to help us write survey questions that are not so subjective?" This industry is hungry for resources that support their efforts to replicate much of what learning and development has accomplished in terms of needs assessment and evaluation work. These needs include resources to help them design and administer surveys and questionnaires.

Survey Basics will follow a similar flow of other books in the *ASTD Basics* series. Key elements of each chapter include:

▶ Chapter learning objectives outline what readers can expect.

▶ "Think About This" sidebars highlight issues, concerns, and problems faced when developing surveys and questionnaires, and in some cases offer exercises so readers can reflect on what they are learning as they read.

▶ "Noted" sidebars reference key points and works by survey design experts.

▶ "Basic Rules" sidebars provide readers guidelines to consider regardless of the purpose of their survey.

▶ "Getting It Done" action steps guide readers toward the development of a survey for a specific project.

At the end of the book, readers will find lists of references, additional resources, list of definitions, and solutions to some of the "Think About This" activities.

How to Use This Book

Survey Basics is intended to serve as a primer on survey design and administration. As previously mentioned, there are many publications that provide more detail on the technical aspects of survey design. This book will give readers a core understanding of the process and how to address some of the issues they run into every day.

To get the most out of the book, we suggest that you read the book in the order it was written. At the end of each chapter, readers will find an action assignment. Ultimately, these assignments will lead readers through the development of a survey for a program or project in which they are involved. However, each chapter stands alone if readers want to focus only on one specific content area.

We suggest that as you read each chapter, reflect on the "Think About This" issues and exercises and refer to the resources listed in the back of the book. One resource you will want to bookmark is the *Social Research Methods Knowledge Base*. This website, developed by Dr. William M. K. Trochim, is one of the most comprehensive online research design resources available.

To support readers, the ROI Institute will work with ASTD to continue the conversation about survey design and administration on the ASTD Evaluation/ROI blog. In addition, ROI Institute offers an online version of their Survey Basics Workshop that they have been offering internally to clients over the past few years.

Look for These Icons

What's Inside This Chapter

Each chapter of the book begins with a preview of the topics discussed in the chapter. You can use this information as a guide for what to expect as well as a quick reference should you wish to jump to a section that interests you most.

Think About This

These sections consist of specific lists, tips, and questions that will help you utilize the techniques and concepts covered in the chapter.

Basic Rules

These rules are short statements that encompass the important and fundamental tenets of technical training development.

Noted

These sections include important additional information that slightly digresses from the regular text.

Getting It Done

This is the final section of each chapter. This section provides a way for you to relate the concepts and principles to your own technical training project.

Acknowledgments

■■

We are excited about the opportunity to develop this book for ASTD and for the learning and development community. Our typical books address measurement, evaluation, and ROI. Most of our books include content on data collection, instrument design, and achieving high response rates. Case study books include examples of instruments used for specific ROI projects. But this is our first book strictly on survey design and administration and we have the publishing team at ASTD to thank for the opportunity. ASTD is a true partner with ROI Institute, and particularly Jack and Patti. The support of the publications team is more than we could ever expect. Their understanding and flexibility when our travels and client demands interfere with progress is greatly appreciated.

We'd like to give special thanks to Justin Brusino, Community of Practice Manager, Learning Technologies, who gave us the initial go-ahead on this project; and to Juana Llorens, Community of Practice Manager, Learning and Development, for agreeing to move forward with this project and for adjusting the project timeline to accommodate us. Also, we'd like to thank Ashley McDonald, Manager, ASTD Press, for taking on another one of our publications.

Many thanks go to Nicole Mallory, manager of publications at the ROI Institute. Nicole juggles our many publications and is skilled at shifting focus on a minute's notice. Finally, we want to acknowledge our clients, workshop participants, and all of the graduate students with whom we work. Many of them encouraged us to move forward with the book. Their interest in measurement, evaluation, and ROI and all that goes into these processes keep us moving forward with refining existing content and creating new content. It is for them that we authored this book.

Patti P. Phillips, PhD
Jack J. Phillips, PhD
Bruce Aaron, PhD

The Basics

What's Inside This Chapter

This chapter describes the basic issues in designing, developing, and administering surveys. Upon completion you should be able to:

▶ Describe different types of surveys
▶ Describe factors that determine the value of a survey
▶ Identify four types of errors found in surveys and how to avoid them
▶ Assess your knowledge of survey design

Surveys Defined

Surveys represent one of the most often used techniques of collecting information from or about people to describe, compare, explain, or predict their knowledge, attitudes, or behaviors (Fink, 2003). Simply put, surveys are a tool used for obtaining needed information. Surveys are used to measure:

▶ employee attitudes
▶ customer satisfaction

- ▶ employee use of training
- ▶ student performance
- ▶ quality of facilitation
- ▶ audience opinions
- ▶ program outcomes.

They are also used to collect data useful in isolating the effects of a program on improvement in business measures; converting data to monetary value; identifying planned actions associated with acquisition of knowledge, skill, or information; and forecasting the return on investing in a particular program or project. Researchers, evaluators, learning and development professionals, HR professionals, meeting planners, and others administer surveys because they want to influence or persuade some audience, create or change an existing program or process, or understand or predict some behavior or outcomes.

The use of surveys has evolved over the past 75 years. Its evolution began with a high level of surveyor-respondent interaction and high level of trust in the survey process. Today, it is a process with low levels of surveyor-respondent interaction and sometimes, even lower levels of trust. For example, in the 1960s people were more readily available to respond to a survey. Travel for work was less prevalent and work hours were structured. An eight-to-five job really meant that the person worked 8:00 a.m. to 5:00 p.m., so the target audience was accessible. If asked to participate in a survey, the individual would willingly oblige, wearing participation as a badge of honor. Survey questions were answered honestly and there was trust that the data would be used appropriately.

Contrast then with now. Working remotely is the new norm and people are less accessible than ever before. Even with the most current technologies, accessibility is a challenge. Most people are not sitting by email in hopes of receiving a survey to complete. Even if they do receive the survey, they are so overwhelmed with email and projects, survey response moves to the bottom of the list. So, accessing potential respondents can be a challenge. In addition, there is a much lower level of trust in the survey process. This leads to either no response or biased responses to avoid conflict (Dillman, et al. 2009).

These changes, among others, have advanced the research around the use of surveys. Books, courses, and resources are available to professionals and students interested in developing and administering surveys as well as interpreting results to make them actionable. Interest in surveys has grown exponentially in the past two decades in the learning and development field. This is due to increased efforts to show results of programs and projects and an increased interest in research data, with which professionals and managers can compare their activities against those of others.

With the evolution of, and growing interest in survey research, there is an equally growing demand for technology that supports surveys. Many conference exhibitors sell products and services that support the use of surveys as a data collection method. These exhibitors exclude all of the survey service providers who have not yet tapped into the learning and development market.

Surveys come in various forms. Statistical surveys include self-administered questionnaires, panel surveys, telephone surveys, and intercept surveys, all of which are used in a variety of industries to easily and inexpensively capture data. Qualitative surveys such as focus groups, interviews, observations, and consensus panels allow researchers to gather a deeper understanding of information than they can get from a self-administered questionnaire.

In the learning and development, human resources, performance improvement, and meetings and events fields, the most common survey instruments are:

- ▶ self-administered surveys and questionnaires
- ▶ interviews
- ▶ focus groups
- ▶ observations.

Self-Administered Surveys and Questionnaires

The self-administered questionnaire is the most commonly used statistical survey in the learning and development, human resources, and meetings and events fields, and the survey to which this book primarily refers. A self-administered questionnaire consists of questions that individual respondents complete by themselves. These surveys are typically delivered in-person while a group is still intact, via postal service or courier service, email, or an established website.

Self-administered questionnaires are considered statistical surveys because the data are typically analyzed using statistical methods. These surveys collect both categorical (qualitative) and numerical (quantitative) data. Self-administered questionnaires also collect verbatim data requiring the use of content analysis to derive meaning from such responses. You will often hear the terms *survey* and *questionnaire* used interchangeably when referring to a self-administered questionnaire. The distinction lies in the type of data collected by the instrument. A survey, in the context of the self-administered questionnaire, often refers to an instrument through which attitudinal data are collected via simple categorical scales; a questionnaire refers to a survey instrument through which more in-depth and numerical data are collected. For example, a questionnaire would include open-ended questions along with questions taking numerical measurements. Table 1-1 presents what is often referred to as a simple survey instrument. Table 1-2 presents what is often referred to as a questionnaire. They are both examples of survey instruments.

Table 1-1. Sample of a Simple Survey

Please provide your reaction to course facilitation using the following scale:

SD = Strongly Disagree
 D = Disagree
 N = Neither Agree Nor Disagree
 A = Agree
SA = Strongly Agree

	SD	D	N	A	SA
1. The instructor was knowledgeable about the subject.	☐	☐	☐	☐	☐
2. The instructor was prepared for the class.	☐	☐	☐	☐	☐
3. Participants were encouraged to take part in class discussions.	☐	☐	☐	☐	☐
4. The instructor effectively answered participants' questions.	☐	☐	☐	☐	☐
5. The instructor's enthusiasm kept the participants actively engaged.	☐	☐	☐	☐	☐
6. The instructor described how I can apply the skills and knowledge taught in the class.	☐	☐	☐	☐	☐

Table 1-2. Sample Questionnaire

Follow-Up Coaching Questions

1. To what extent did coaching positively influence the following measures:

	Significant Influence				No Influence	
	5	4	3	2	1	n/a
Productivity	☐	☐	☐	☐	☐	☐
Sales	☐	☐	☐	☐	☐	☐
Quality	☐	☐	☐	☐	☐	☐
Cost	☐	☐	☐	☐	☐	☐
Efficiency	☐	☐	☐	☐	☐	☐
Time	☐	☐	☐	☐	☐	☐
Employee satisfaction	☐	☐	☐	☐	☐	☐
Customer satisfaction	☐	☐	☐	☐	☐	☐

2. What other measures were positively influenced by coaching?

_____

3. Of the measures listed above, improvement in which one is most directly linked to coaching? (Check only one.)

   ☐ productivity   ☐ sales   ☐ quality

   ☐ cost   ☐ efficiency   ☐ time

   ☐ employee satisfaction   ☐ customer satisfaction

4. Please define the measure above and its unit for measurement.

_____

5. How much did the measure identified in questions 3 and 4 improve since you began this process?
   _____   ☐ weekly   ☐ monthly   ☐ annually

6. What other processes, programs, or events may have contributed to this improvement?

_____

7. Recognizing that other factors may have caused this improvement, estimate the percent of improvement related directly to coaching.
   _____ %

8. For this measure, what is the monetary value of improvement for one unit of this measure? Although this is difficult, please make every effort to estimate the value.

_____

9. Please state your basis for the estimated value of improvement you indicated above.

_____

10. What is the annual value of improvement in the measure you selected above?

_____

11. What confidence do you place in the estimates you have provided in the prior questions?
    0% is no confidence, 100% is certainty.
    _____ %

Self-administered surveys and questionnaires are the survey instrument of choice for many reasons, including:

- **Quantity of data:** A large amount of data can be collected from a large number of respondents. There is no limit to the number of questions you can ask on this type of survey instrument, other than that imposed by respondents. Too many questions often lead to unanswered questions.

- **Cost of data collection:** In comparison to interviews, focus groups—and, in some cases—observations, the self-administered questionnaire is the least-costly survey instrument.

- **Ease of administration:** Once developed, the self-administered questionnaire is distributed to all potential respondents. While it is important to put a plan into place to ensure a successful response rate, as described in chapter 6, administration of this survey instrument is relatively simple.

- **Utility of data:** Given the right questions are asked in the right way, data obtained through the self-administered questionnaire can be used in a variety of ways. Improving programs, benchmarking against similar organizations, forecasting future outcomes, and providing facilitator feedback are just a few examples of uses for data from questionnaires.

- **Time to develop and administer:** While it is important to spend time planning the questionnaire, the overall time to develop and administer a questionnaire is minimal compared to that of other techniques.

- **Time requirement of respondent:** Compared to other techniques, respondents usually spend less time completing a self-administered questionnaire than when participating in interviews or focus groups, and are, therefore, often more willing to do so.

- **Accuracy of data:** There is no guarantee that a person will respond objectively to a survey question collected on any type of survey instrument. However, when developed, administered, and analyzed appropriately, a self-administered questionnaire can generate information with a high level of reliability.

While using self-administered surveys and questionnaires can provide information based on a lot of data from a lot of people, it is limiting in a number of ways. For example, if you want clarification of a particular response, you are likely to have to ask the respondent or otherwise, accept the data at hand. Also, if a respondent has a concern about one of your survey questions, they are likely to either respond based on their limited understanding or not respond at all. To develop this type of survey, you must know up front what information you want to gather. Sometimes, you don't know what you don't know, which is problematic if you want to develop a statistical survey such as the self-administered survey or questionnaire.

Noted

While a self-administered questionnaire collects data that are often analyzed with statistics, it does not mean that the data are purely objective. Statistical surveys are used to collect subjective, perception data. The types of questions asked lend themselves to a higher level of statistical analysis than those typically used in qualitative surveys described below, but the questions and subsequent responses are often based on perception.

Interviews

Interviews are conversations between two or more people where one person (the interviewer) is asking questions to gather specific information from another (the interviewee[s]). While the interviewer goes into the interview with a specific set of questions, additional questions may arise during the conversation as the interviewee provides information and basis for further probing. Interviews are an excellent method of collecting data when identifying business and performance needs. They are a good technique to probe for information, particularly regarding a sensitive topic. Interview data complement or enhance data derived from a self-administered questionnaire.

Interviews can be costly, given the time commitment required of both the interviewer and the interviewee. The number of questions asked is limited to the time available for the interviews, thereby reducing the number of questions asked. Scheduling the interview can be a challenge, given the inaccessibility of individuals. The use of telephone versus face-to-face interviews helps reduce costs, particularly those associated with travel; however, time, availability, and quantity of data are still issues. Interviews are important in the surveying process, but their use is selective.

According to Marrelli (2010) interviewers should develop an interview protocol to ensure all required information is collected and that data collection is consistent when using multiple interviewers. Interview protocols should include instructions to be read by the interviewer(s), space for demographic data, the specific survey questions, a closing statement, and space for the interviewer to record interviewee responses (both verbal and nonverbal). Table 1-3 is a sample interview protocol.

Table 1-3. Sample Interview Protocol

Interview for the "Giving Employees Useful Feedback" Course Evaluation

Interviewer Name:

Interviewee Name: Phone Number:

Work Unit: Years of Work Experience:

Interview Date and Time:

Instructions to interviewer are in italics:

Opening Statement

Read the following statement to the interviewee:

Hello, [name]. My name is....*[Take a moment here for small talk to build rapport.]* We are talking to a sample of the employees of the managers who recently participated in the "Giving Employees Useful Feedback" course to find out if they are applying what they learned in class on the job. The information you provide will be kept confidential. It will only be seen by the evaluation analysts who will summarize the data for all employees. This information will help us improve the training course.

I will ask you several questions about the feedback your manager has given you in the last month. Depending on your responses, the interview will take from 5 to 30 minutes. We are defining feedback as information about your performance that explains what you did well or how you could improve. Feedback can range from a few words as your manager passes you in the hall to a long discussion in her office.

Questions

Ask the interviewee the following questions and note the responses below each question.

1. In the last month, has your manager given you feedback?:

       Circle employee's response: Yes   No

2. Did you request feedback from your manager in the last month?

       Circle employee's response: Yes   No

If the employee responded "no" to both questions 1 and 2, skip to the closing statement.

If the employee responds "yes" to question 2 , ask:

2a: Approximately how many times did you ask the manager for feedback?

2b: Please describe the situations in which you asked for feedback.

Proceed with question 3 if the employee responded "yes" to question 1. Otherwise, skip to the closing statement.

3. How would you rate the helpfulness of the feedback your manager has given you in the past month?

____ Very helpful   ____ Helpful   ____ Somewhat helpful   ____ Not helpful   ____ Harmful

4. Please describe the most helpful feedback your manager has given you in the past month. As best as you can remember, tell me about the situation and what the manager said.

5. Why did you find this feedback especially helpful?

(Note: Additional questions would appear here.)

Closing Statement

Read the following statement to the interviewee:

This is the conclusion of the interview. Thank you for taking the time to help us improve managerial training. Your input is valuable. We will present the results of the interviews to the executive team next month.

Source: Marrelli, A. F. (2010). Conducting Interviews. In Phillips, P.P., ed., *ASTD Handbook of Measuring and Evaluating Training.* Alexandria: ASTD Press.

Noted

Studies from a variety of fields report that telephone interviews are somewhat equally reliable as face-to-face interviews (Blankenship, 2009; Irvine, 2010; Starr et al., 1999). Specific differences include:

- Face-to-face interviews tend to be longer.
- Participants talk more frequently during face-to-face interviews.
- Participants talk longer before the interviewer asks another question during face-to-face interviews.
- Interviewers tend to interrupt the participant more often, assuming the participant has completed his thoughts during telephone interviews.
- Respondents sometimes report feeling more skeptical about the survey when responding to telephone interviews.

Focus Groups

Focus groups are another useful type of survey in that they offer the opportunity to survey multiple respondents, but in a controlled environment where respondents can hear what others have to say. Focus groups are similar to interviews in that there is an interviewer, otherwise referred to as a facilitator, and there are interviewees, referred to as focus group participants. The difference is that in an interview, even group interviews, group interaction is not an important part of the process. In a focus group, the facilitator will ask specific questions of each participant, but in addition to the individual response, group interaction will assist in data generation.

Focus groups are useful when it is important for respondents to hear comments from others. For example, focus groups have been used to convert improvement in business measures as a result of a training program to money. They have also been used to identify the barriers and enablers of learning transfer. Structured focus groups, such as nominal-group technique, are useful when investigating why an event is occurring, such as employee turnover (Phillips and Edwards, 2009).

The key to a successful focus group is to keep it focused, while allowing for group interaction. Giving each person a specific amount of time to share his thoughts is critical. As in the case of interviews, establishing a protocol will help ensure consistent facilitation of the focus group. It will also help ensure you leave the focus group with the information you set out to collect. Table 1-4 presents a focus group protocol for an emergency response program along with a sample layout of a focus group notepad (Phillips and Phillips, 2005). It is helpful to invite someone to take notes, even if you plan to record the focus group. The focus group notepad shown in Table 1-4 offers the recorder an opportunity to take detailed notes as well as note key points made during the focus group session.

Focus groups can be expensive to run. With an ideal participation of eight to 12 people, multiple focus groups are often needed to gather data reliable enough to make decisions. Therefore, focus groups are often used to supplement other data collection techniques.

Table 1-4. Focus Group Protocol and Sample Notepad for a Study Conducted on an Emergency Response Support Program

Focus Groups Facilitator Protocol

Purpose

This focus group is intended to help us understand how knowledge and skills gained in the program have been applied (Level 3).

During the focus group you will identify effectiveness with application, frequency of application, barriers, and enablers to application.

What to Do

1. Give yourself extra time.
2. Arrive a few minutes early to prepare the room.
3. Introduce yourself to the point of contact. Reinforce the purpose, and explain the process.
4. Set up the room so that the tables or chairs are in a u-shape so that participants can see each other and you can become part of the group.
5. Place tent cards at each seat.
6. As participants arrive, introduce yourself, give them refreshments, and chat a few minutes.
7. As you ask questions, write the answers, but don't try to write every word. Listen for key issues. Listen for quotes that are meaningful and make important points that reinforce use of knowledge and skills.
8. When you have gathered the information you need, thank each participant. Clean up; thank your point of contact. Leave.
9. Find a place to debrief with your partner and clarify notes. Do it immediately, because you will surely forget something.
10. When you return, analyze the data.

What to Take

1. Map.
2. Point of contact telephone numbers.
3. Tent cards. Each tent card should have a number in a corner. Participants can write their first name just so you call them by name, but your notes will refer to the participant number.
4. Refreshments—something light, but a treat of some kind because people respond to food, and it relaxes the environment.
5. Flipchart.
6. Markers for the tent cards and the flipchart.
7. Focus group notepads. A tape or digital recorder is the ideal data collection instrument, but it also intimidates people.
8. An umbrella.

What to Wear

You will be in a comfortable environment, so ties and high heels are not necessary, but do dress professionally. No jeans and tennis shoes: business casual.

What to Say

The intent is to understand how participants are applying what they learned during training. Start on time. You do not want to keep the participants over the allotted time.

1. Thank everyone for participating.
2. Introduce yourself and your partner. Tell them you are part of a research team conducting a study on the program. Reinforce with them that their input is important to this study. The results of the study will be used to improve training and other program support initiatives.
3. Share the purpose of the focus group.
4. Explain how the process will work and that their input is strictly confidential.
5. Have them put their first name on the tent card. Explain that the numbers in the corner of the tent card are for recording purposes and that in no way will their name be recorded. Explain that after the focus groups you and your partner will compile notes; your notes will be later compiled with those of the other focus groups. Also, tell them that their input in the focus group is supplemental to a questionnaire that they may have already received.
6. Begin question 1 with participant 1.

Questions

Each person will answer each question before moving to the next question. The idea is to allow each person to hear what the others say so that they can reflect on their responses. We don't want groupthink. We want to know what each individual thinks.

Q1. Now that you have had a chance to apply what you learned regarding your emergency response duties, how effectively have you been able to execute those duties?

Q2. What specific barriers have interfered with your ability to execute your duties?

Q3: What has supported your efforts?

Focus Group Notepad	
Question:	
Notes	Notable Quote

Date:
Location:
Facilitator: Page ___ of ___

Noted

It is important not to confuse types of surveys with types of data. Self-administered questionnaires collect quantitative and qualitative data. Qualitative surveys collect qualitative data and can be used to collect quantitative data.

Observations

Observations require that one or more individuals watch people in action in natural settings, such as their offices. Structured forms are used so observers can record their opinions and thoughts of what they observe. Video and audio recordings are sometimes made so the observer can replay them and make further observations, and also retain a record of the behaviors observed. Observations are useful for assessing an employee's ability to follow tasks or perform at a specified level and to gauge their routine behavior over a period of time.

Development of a reliable observation checklist or a behaviorally anchored numerical scale to measure observed performance takes time. It is important that measurement tools are developed so that if two or more observers are assessing the same individual or entity (document, video or audio recording), they report the same results. Reliability, or the lack thereof, of observations is one of the top concerns when using this survey technique.

Think About This

Below are scenarios describing the use of questionnaires, interviews, focus groups, and observations.

Questionnaire

The front desk staff at a major hotel has participated in a program to teach them how to use a new reservation system that is being installed. As part of the evaluation, it is important to obtain reactions to the program and capture planned actions and a forecast of success.

Interview

Supervisors attended a problem-solving program in which they learned a logical approach to solving significant problems facing their work units. As a part of the evaluation of the program, the HR staff needs feedback from participants concerning their use of the acquired skills. The staff thinks there is a possibility of a success story here and will need to probe for details.

Focus Group

Intact team members are involved in a conflict resolution program where they acquired skills to resolve conflicts and disputes among themselves. Team members in this work group have a high degree of interaction and some responsibilities include checking the work of others. There had been an unusually high level of friction with displays of open conflicts in the group. In the program, participants learned how to deal with these issues and work together as a smooth operating team. The HR staff needs to collect information about the group's progress with skills, ideally in an environment where there is an opportunity for group members to listen to comments from others.

Observation

Customer service representatives have learned to resolve customer complaints in the most effective manner. An integral part of the program required customer service representatives to follow a series of planned steps to resolve the complaints, using empathy and listening skills. As part of the evaluation, the HR staff must determine the extent to which participants are actually utilizing the newly-acquired skills.

The Value of a Survey

A survey sets out to: describe, compare, explain, or predict a condition, behavior, or outcome. It provides stakeholders information they need to make decisions about programs, projects, people, and initiatives. How much you should invest in a survey to accomplish these purposes depends on the value of the information derived from that survey.

Value of survey information is determined by (Alreck, 2003):

- information sought by the client
- costs associated with making a wrong decision
- amount of uncertainty given a pending decision or action
- reduction of uncertainty by the survey.

Information Sought by the Client

Key stakeholders are interested in a variety of data. For example, when it comes to the value of the learning and development investment, CEOs are interested in seeing improvement in measures such as business impact and ROI (Phillips and Phillips, 2010). Other stakeholders may be interested in how well program participants apply what they learn. Still others are interested in how participants react to facilitation and design of content.

A survey is valuable if it provides the information sought by the client. There may be additional data collected using the survey instrument, but their investment in the survey will be less if the client information is nonexistent. For example, in a large retail store chain, senior executives were interested in how much sales increased as a result of a pilot off-the-shelf training program in which 48 salespeople participated. Sales data were available through performance records, so access to information was relatively easy. To ensure the program affected behavior on the job, the learning and development team wanted to conduct a survey.

Because the target audience was retail salespeople, the learning and development team considered hiring mystery shoppers to observe the sales team's behavior. This is a classic approach to measuring application of knowledge and skills in the retail industry. Because the senior executives were most interested in sales, they knew the level of investment required for mystery shoppers was well beyond that which executives would make. They also knew that supervisors could provide only a limited perspective, so they decided to administer a survey to the participants themselves. This less expensive approach provided data suitable for their purposes and was acceptable to the executives (Phillips and Phillips, 2010b).

Cost of Making a Wrong Decision

Survey information is used to make decisions. Those decisions may be to expand a program, eliminate a program, promote individuals, offer individuals opportunity for development, launch a new program, or implement a new learning management system. The list is enormous. The cost of making the wrong decision varies depending on the type of decision. For example, if a senior manager decides to roll out a new off-the-shelf sales training program and the program proves ineffective, there is a direct cost to her decision. On the other hand, if she decides not to move forward with the program, and the program could have had a significant impact on sales, that lost opportunity has actual value.

A survey that can help reduce or avoid costs or lost profits associated with making a wrong decision is a valuable survey. The investment in that survey must be relative to the cost it can help avoid or the profit it can help gain.

Amount of Uncertainty Given a Pending Decision

Along with the actual costs of making a wrong decision, there exists uncertainty. Occasionally, decision makers will have already narrowed their options, but a level of uncertainty exists in deciding which of the options is best. For example, a decision is going to be made to purchase a new learning management system (LMS). Two options exist, but decision makers just cannot come to terms with which one of the two systems is best for the organization. A survey that can help decision makers choose between two or more alternatives is a valuable survey.

Degree of Uncertainty Reduction

A final consideration when placing value on a survey is the degree to which the survey information can reduce uncertainty. For example, a manager may be uncertain as to how the new contact management system is working for her call center representatives. A survey can reduce that uncertainty by asking the right questions of the customer service representatives. On the other hand, a manager may want to forecast the impact of a new contact management system before making the purchase in an effort to reduce the uncertainty she has that the purchase is a good funding decision. A survey can help reduce that uncertainty.

Basic Rule
Never invest more in a survey than the benefits of the information it generates.

Error in Surveys

Regardless of the type of survey, there will always be some level of error. The key is to develop your survey instrument and its administration plan so that you can minimize the error. According to Dillman (2009), there are four types of potential errors. They are:

- ▶ coverage error
- ▶ sampling error
- ▶ non-response error
- ▶ measurement error.

Coverage Error

Coverage error occurs when you have selected the wrong respondent group and when all members of your targeted group do not have an equal opportunity to participate in the survey. For example, you might decide to administer a survey to gather information about how employees perceive the learning and development function in terms of serving their needs. In order to avoid costs, you decide to use one of many online survey tools. However, many members of the field staff are located in remote areas where Internet is unreliable, if existent at all. By moving forward with your online survey, you will be making a conscious decision to ignore the opinions of some of the field staff. You are limiting your coverage, thereby, increasing your error.

As you will read in chapter 6, by using multiple modes of delivery you can open up the opportunity to all potential respondents.

Sampling Error

Sampling error occurs when only a subset of your population is targeted for response rather than the entire population. By surveying only a subset of your population, you are immediately interjecting error into your results. This is also known as selection bias.

For example, you want to measure the company's employee engagement. To avoid costs, you administer the survey only to a portion of your employees. You have now biased your results to that small group. With a large enough sample you can make statistical inferences based on your limited data, but the reliability of those inferences depends on population size, homogeneity of the population, confidence interval (margin of error), and confidence level. Chapter 5 addresses these issues and more regarding the topic of sampling.

Non-Response Error

Non-response error occurs when people selected for the survey who do not respond are different from those who do respond in a way that is important to the survey project. For example, a research organization wants to know the opinion of its members regarding a variety of program evaluation processes. The results would have a significant amount of non-response error if actual users of those evaluation processes were less likely to respond than managers of the users (who are less familiar with the processes). Ensuring a successful response from your targeted audience is critical for credible results.

Measurement Error

The final type of error is measurement error. Measurement error occurs when the wrong questions are asked or when the right questions are asked in the wrong way. Poorly worded questions, survey distribution mode, respondent attitudes, and behaviors can affect measurement error. For example, the following question appears on the end-of-course evaluation for a two-day workshop:

Please indicate the extent to which you agree with the following:
1 = Disagree; 5 = Agree

The content and facilitation of the course was satisfactory.   1   2   3   4   5

What is wrong with this question? If you suggest that there are two questions in one, you are correct. Barreling is a common error found in survey questions. How questions are written and the scales applied are important considerations when trying to manage measurement error. Chapters 2, 3, and 4 cover topics associated with measurement error.

Characteristics of an Effective Survey

Regardless of the type of survey instrument you plan to employ, there are certain characteristics surveys must meet. They are:

- ▶ measurable survey objectives
- ▶ sound research design
- ▶ effective survey question design
- ▶ sound sampling strategy, when needed
- ▶ effective survey response strategy
- ▶ meaningful data summary
- ▶ effective data display and reporting.

Each of these criteria is presented in more detail throughout the book, but a brief summary of the criteria is presented here.

Survey Objectives

Survey objectives are the basis for all things about the survey. Survey objectives represent the need for the questions as well as the measures to be taken through the survey instrument. By reading the survey objectives, a surveyor should be able to identify the measures (or variables) as well as how best to collect the data. Good survey objectives also provide insight into the research design.

Survey objectives come in three forms: 1) a statement, 2) a question, or 3) a hypothesis. Because many surveys are used for descriptive purposes, the statement is the most common survey objective. However, there are times when a research question is an appropriate survey objective, particularly when the survey is intended to identify key issues that will ultimately form the basis for a larger survey. Hypotheses are special-purpose objectives and are, technically, only used when the theory the survey is testing is based on enough evidence to justify hypothesis testing; although, specific, measurable, achievable, relevant, and time-bound (SMART) program objectives set for learning and development initiatives are written much like hypotheses. You will read more about survey objectives in chapter 2.

Research Design

Research design refers to how the survey will be administered in terms of targeted groups, comparisons of data to multiple groups, and frequency of survey administration. Many survey projects represent cross-sectional studies. In a cross-sectional design, a survey is administered to a group at a defined time. For example, you may decide to measure your employees' overall satisfaction with their jobs. This measurement of satisfaction for the group at this particular time is a cross-sectional survey.

On the other hand, you may want to compare the change in behavior as measured by a 360-degree feedback survey between one group involved in a program and another group not involved in a program. This comparison of two groups falls into the experimental (randomly selected participants) or quasi-experimental (non-randomly selected participants) designs. Occasionally you will not know the specific questions to ask on a self-administered questionnaire. If that is the case, you can use a focus group (qualitative survey) to gather preliminary information that will inform the questionnaire. Or, you may administer a broad-based survey to capture data on key issues, but you use those data to guide questions asked during a focus group. These mixed method research designs are increasing in popularity and provide a robust foundation for collecting relevant data. Chapter 3 presents more detail on research design.

Survey Question Design

A quote by Ernst Cassirer, a Jewish German historian and philosopher, opens chapter 1 of the book *Historians' Fallacies* by David Hackett Fischer (Harper-Perennial, 1970). It reads:

> *Are we to be disgusted with science because it has not fulfilled our hopes or redeemed its promises? And are we, for this reason, to announce the "bankruptcy" of science, as is so often and so flippantly done? But this is rash and foolish; for we can hardly blame science just because we have not asked the right questions.*

Right there—in a few brief words Cassirer captures the essence of survey question design. All too often we make decisions based on results derived from the wrong questions. Even if they are the right questions, if they are poorly written the outcome is the same: decisions based on bad questions.

Survey question design is the heart of survey research. Asking the right questions the right way to the right people in the context of an appropriate research framework generates relevant, useable information. But how do we know what are the right questions? We refer to the survey objectives. How do we know we are asking them the right way? Read chapter 4.

Sampling

Sampling is a process developed to avoid costs of sending out one more survey, while allowing assumptions to be made to nonrespondents of a population. While it is a common practice in large general population studies, marketing research, and opinion polling, its use is limited within the organization setting. This is particularly true when evaluating learning and development programs, human resources initiatives, and large meetings or events. But, when needed, a sound sampling strategy is an imperative in order to reduce error when making inferences. Because sampling is part of a sound research design, content on this topic is found in chapter 3.

Survey Response

An effective survey administration strategy will help ensure you receive an acceptable quantity and quality of responses. Research describes a variety of incentives and processes available to us to increase our chances of getting a good response rate. Chapter 6 describes these opportunities as well as the research that supports them.

Data Summary

Data "summary" is a less intimidating way of referring to data "analysis." However, if you collect survey data, whether with a statistical survey or an interview, you will analyze the data. But fear not, it does not have to be difficult. Many of the surveys used in learning and development, human resources, and meetings and events lend themselves to simple descriptive statistics. While many organizations are advancing their capability in more complex analytics, most survey data captured for the purposes of conducting needs assessments and program evaluations can be summarized using basic statistical procedures. Credible qualitative analysis can be done by simply categorizing words into themes. Chapter 7 provides a brief look at how to summarize your survey results so that they are meaningful and useful. A future book on data analysis basics will address more detail on analysis for the learning and development, HR, and meetings and events professional.

Data Display and Reporting

A final characteristic of a good survey is one for which the final results are reported in such a way that stakeholders immediately "get it." Reporting results requires written words, oral presentations, and effective graphical displays. Along with data summary, chapter 7 provides tips on how to effectively report your survey results.

Ethical Considerations

Survey design and administration is a balance between art and science. The artistic side includes developing creative ways to ask questions, encourage response, and present results. The science side requires ensuring you ask the right questions, avoid error, and administer the survey in such a way that it meets the culture and philosophy of your organization. Adding to the balance is ethics.

If you are working in a government or academic institution and you plan to administer a survey, your Institutional Review Board (IRB) has a list of procedures for you to follow. However, if you are working in a business or an organization for which IRB is not required, it is still incumbent on you to maintain an ethical posture as you employ survey methods.

Here are a few basic ethical standards to follow:

1. Protect the best interest of your client by taking on the fiduciary responsibility of resources. All too often we spend too much on a survey that is of less value than the resources spent. Remember: All roads lead to ROI. Invest in the survey based on the value of the information it generates.

2. Get permission to publish survey results. While you may be proud of your work, ask permission of your client and the respondents before you make the results public.

3. Remember, the survey and subsequent results are the property of the client. Treat them that way.

4. Refuse any project for which the client wants to impose bias in order to get certain results. Misrepresenting results just to get a paycheck is unacceptable.

5. Refrain from imposing your own bias just to satisfy the client.

6. Keep respondent identity confidential and anonymous if promised at the onset of the survey project. Often confidentiality is perceived to be a more reliable promise than anonymity. But whatever you promise, keep it.

7. To the best of your ability, never allow the client to use results to reprimand respondents. Misuse of data is one of the greatest concerns of potential survey respondents.

8. Use the appropriate type of analysis. Creative statistics are interesting and often slip right by the integrity police, so take care to analyze data appropriately.

Basic Rule
Misrepresenting results just to get a paycheck is unacceptable.

Getting It Done

Now that you have been introduced to a few key concepts about surveys, develop a baseline of your survey expertise. Using the Survey Knowledge Scorecard shown in Table 1-5, rate yourself in terms of how much you know about the concepts listed. The scale you will use is a 0 to 5 scale with 0 meaning you know nothing about the content area; and 5 meaning you know all there is to know. There are 20 content areas, so the highest possible score you can receive is 100 points. Complete the survey now, then after you complete the book to see if your score improves. Once you have your post-reading score, develop an action plan to learn more.

Table 1-5. Survey Knowledge Scorecard

For each content area, score yourself 0 – 5. Zero (0) means you know nothing about the content area. Five (5) means you know all there is to know. Note your ratings on each item and your total score. Once you have your post-reading score, develop an action plan to improve.

| I know nothing | 0 | 1 | 2 | 3 | 4 | 5 | I know it all |

Content Area	Score (0-5)
1. Types of surveys	
2. Types of errors found in surveys	
3. Ethical considerations when administering surveys	
4. Types of survey objectives	
5. How to write SMART objectives	
6. Experimental research designs	
7. Descriptive research designs	
8. Writing quality survey questions (the stem)	
9. Writing quality response choices (the scale)	
10. Different types of survey scales	
11. Types of sampling procedures	
12. How to calculate sample size	
13. When to calculate sample size	
14. Techniques to ensure high response	
15. Descriptive statistics	
16. Measures of central tendency	
17. Importance of measuring variance	
18. Standard values like coefficient of variation and z-score	
19. Writing up the final report	
20. Graphical displays of data	
Total Score	

Highest possible score: 100 points   **Your score:** _____ **points**

2

Survey Objectives

████ ████ ████ ████ ████ ████ ████ ████ ████ ████ ████ ████

What's Inside This Chapter

This chapter describes the importance of
objectives in developing your survey.
Upon completion you should be able to:

► Describe the three types of survey objectives
► Develop measurable survey objectives
► Identify information needs necessary to measure objectives
► Develop an objectives map that translates broad objectives
to specific measures

The Need for Surveys

Just as learning objectives set the stage for a successful program and its subsequent
evaluation, survey objectives set the stage for an effective survey research project. In
many cases, program objectives and survey objectives are one and the same.

An objective is a statement of the survey's expected outcomes (Fink, 2002).
Survey objectives are the basis for the survey questions. They define the kind of

information that is needed and often lead the survey designer toward the appropriate survey instrument, research design, source of data, and timing for data collection. By developing clear, measurable survey objectives, you increase your chances that the resulting information is valuable to stakeholders.

Survey objectives come from a stated need. This need can be a problem identified by an executive, an opportunity identified by one of the learning and development staff, a concern from an employee, a document, or a set of reports. Surveys serve the need to observe people, conditions, output from processes, and other phenomena.

For example, executives of a large car rental agency initiated a leadership development program, but also required that the learning and development team show the return on investment in the program. The program was offered to 36 business unit team leaders and managers across the entire organization, all of whom had specific measures to improve as a result of the program. This generated the need for a survey.

Leaders of a large pharmaceutical manufacturer noticed an increase in the monthly replacement cost of syringes. This generated the need to take a sample survey of the rejected syringes to determine if there was a problem with the product or if there was an opportunity to help quality inspectors improve their ability to designate a syringe as acceptable versus unacceptable.

A regional bank had a significantly higher number of turnover statistics than the benchmark rate of similar banking institutions. The tangible and intangible costs of such high turnover was greater than executives would tolerate. The use of focus groups allowed the human resources department to survey employees to determine why their colleagues were leaving the bank.

Sometimes a general interest or desire to help improve a condition or contribute to the academic or professional literature serves as the need for a survey. Every year, many doctoral candidates employ surveys as their research tool of choice. But to develop a survey requires more than an identified need or general interest. It starts with a set of clear objectives.

From Need to Objectives

Surveys begin with an identified need, but they evolve through the use of objectives. Just as reaction, learning, application, and impact objectives serve as the blueprint for a learning program, objectives serve as the blueprint for survey design. Developing these specific objectives is not necessarily as easy as some might think. It requires some level of research to ensure the right measures are taken through the survey instrument given the time and resources available.

Noted

Gallup's Q^{12} is one of the world's most noted surveys of employee engagement. While it only includes 12 five-point scale survey questions, Q^{12} is based on more than 30 years of quantitative and qualitative research.

Source: Harter, et al. (2006)

Record Reviews

A good starting point to identify objectives for a survey is to access records related to the need. For example, if the boss comes to you and says, *"We have too much employee turnover. Survey our employees to find out why,"* a first step might be to work with HR to review the turnover data so you know the rate at which people are leaving, as well as who is leaving. Then you might look into the exit interview data to determine what people leaving say about their experience in the organization. If the company administers an annual employee satisfaction survey, take a look at those data to determine what indicators of employee frustration exist.

Organizations have a variety of records from which you can gather information to more narrowly focus a broadly observed need. There are quality reports, test data, marketing data, safety and health reports, scorecards, and dashboards. These resources will help you formulate the problem or opportunity in more specific terms and set a direction for your survey project.

Literature Reviews

Sometimes, record reviews describe only part of the story, so you might want to dig deeper. Albeit conducting literature reviews sounds somewhat academic and time consuming, it is a process through which we often go. Reviewing existing research can enlighten you on the appropriate measures you need to take given the purpose of your survey; but it can also disclose the gaps in the literature, giving you the opportunity to add information that will close those gaps. A literature review begins with that broad research question or topic (for example, *"We have too much employee turnover. Survey our employees to find out why."*), and then progressively narrows to the point that you identify the specific objectives you intend to address. Here are some tips to conducting a literature review.

Gather Background Information

Start gathering background information on your topic. While you may have gathered some background information reviewing organizational records, it is still wise to consider how others define the issues you are facing. This step may include the use of dictionaries, textbooks, or searches using your favorite search engine. This step helps you get clear on the definitions and vocabulary associated with your topic. It is at this stage when you also get clear on the specific issues of interest that relate to the broad topic, which, in our example, is employee turnover.

Map Issues to Sources

Next, start mapping specific sources of information for the issues associated with the topic. For example, if your topic is employee turnover, one specific issue of interest may be the cost of turnover. Databases housing peer-reviewed research are good sources of information on this issue, so you might search a database like EBSCOhost or LexisNexis to find articles relevant to the issue at hand. Google Scholar is another good source to lead you to research articles and abstracts. There you can find reference to journals such as *Cornell Hotel and Restaurant Administration* (which published an interesting study on the cost of turnover in the hospitality industry), *Journal of Applied Psychology, International Journal of Human Resource Management,* and more. And don't forget books. Information on issues related to your topic may be available in the business press. Use Amazon.com or other online booksellers as search engines to find books providing relevant information.

The point of this step is to start organizing your information and the relevant sources. This will come in handy when you start developing your objectives.

Read With a Critical Eye

Reading interactively versus passively offers the greatest opportunity to differentiate the relevant from irrelevant literature. Julian Meltzoff (1998) suggests that after reading, the passive reader "may have some general impression of the research and some points of agreement or contention." However, the interactive reader "anticipates what is to come and then discovers whether these expectancies are met along the way" (p. 9). This means that when reading a research article, case study, book, and so on, do so with a clear sense of that for which you are looking. As you read, consider the following questions:

- What is the fundamental premise or problem that this piece of information is addressing?
- What do the authors say? What don't they say?
- If you are reading results of a research report, are the results telling the entire story?
- In what context are the results developed?
- What approaches or methods were used?
- How credible are the sources of information?

Meltzoff (1998) suggests that when reviewing existing research look for key characteristics that support the viability of the study. Below are some of those characteristics.

- Research questions guide the literature review conducted for the study.
- Literature review and statement of the problem inform the research objectives.
- Objectives set up the research design.
- Research objectives, design, type of data dictate the method of data analysis.
- Analysis of the data influences the kinds of conclusions, inferences, and generalizations made by the research.

By paying attention to these characteristics and by keeping a statement describing the need for your project in front of you, you can more quickly eliminate sources that provide only cursory information than if you passively take in the information.

Think About This

As you conduct your literature review, keep in mind the context in which you are working. Business journals and books with a balance of academic research are acceptable sources of information for most corporate and government entities. If your research is occurring in the academic setting, emphasis on peer-reviewed journals tends to be required, but including non-peer reviewed sources is not typically prohibited. Note: *Wikipedia* is an unacceptable source in most academic settings.

Summarize Your Findings

As you read, take notes about your findings. We (the authors) use a variety of tools to make notes of key findings from the literature—including sticky notes, mind mapping, and pocket dictators. Bring your notes together into a summary of findings. Skill with content analysis is helpful here, but not necessary. You will review your notes and look for common themes and issues. While challenging for major projects, this synthesis of information demonstrates your complete understanding of the issue at hand and ensures you target the right objectives and measures for your survey project. As you summarize your findings, be sure to cite your sources. Sources of information provide a foundation for your findings and a premise for the argument you make for moving forward with the stated objectives.

A literature review adds clarity to what you already know and brings you new information. Through this process you will have greater awareness of meanings, methods, and measures associated with your topic; and you will be in a better position to develop measurable, relevant survey objectives that will guide your survey project.

Focus Groups

Another approach to defining the survey objectives is through the use of focus groups. Focus groups, a form of surveying, can provide a wealth of information and serve as a primer for survey development. It is important with a focus group to make sure the right people are in the room. To do so, a fundamental question to ask is, *Who knows best about this topic and relevant measures?* Given the answer, gather eight to 12 of those people together and discuss the overall goal for the survey. Ask three or four pertinent questions and listen to participants as they describe the information you need to collect and the types of questions you should ask on your survey.

In the turnover example, the people who know best why there is a high rate of turnover are, of course, the people who left. Given that they are not readily available to participate in the focus group, you ask their proxy—the people who are still with the organization that represent the demographic of employees who left. To manage potential exposure of the reasons they might want to leave the organization, you ask them to describe the reasons why their colleagues have left. This approach takes the attention off their reasons for potentially leaving while giving them the opportunity to tell you why they would leave, but behind the mask of those who did. Then ask them to rank the reasons to help you sort through the issues on which you need to focus.

By including these individuals as part of your focus group, you not only get a good idea of why people leave, but also the solutions that might have kept them. With this information in hand, you can now develop objectives that will guide development of a survey that can be administered to other employees, validating the findings from the focus group.

Consensus Panels

Consensus panels represent a structured process of gathering data and solving problems. Similar to a focus group, a consensus panel usually consists of a small number of people. It is different, however, in that a focus group explores issues in a structured manner over the course of no more than two hours per group. A consensus panel requires multiple rounds where experts in the area of concern give in-depth information about an issue. This process may include presenting experts with information and having them rank or rate the information against a set of measures on one day. On the second day, experts discuss their ratings from round one, and rate the measures a second time to validate initial perceptions. While there are no absolute requirements in terms of conducting a consensus panel, typically the process includes the identification of experts, a first round of data collection and analysis, and a second round of discussion, data collection, and analysis.

To use a consensus panel to help develop objectives, identify approximately 10 experts in the area of interest, such as employee turnover. It may also be helpful to include experts in survey research. In round one, provide experts with a list of potential survey objectives that have been developed based on your cursory investigation of why turnover is a problem. Ask each expert to rate each objective on its importance and the feasibility of obtaining honest answers to questions pertaining to the objective. At the end of the session, summarize the results from round one.

During round two, present the results to the experts. Discuss the ratings for each objective with them. Then, ask the experts to rate each objective on its importance and the feasibility of obtaining honest answers to questions pertaining to the objective. At the conclusion of the round, summarize the data. The objectives which the most people rank the highest in terms of importance and feasibility of obtaining an honest answer to a question related to the objective, become your survey objectives (Fink, 2003a).

Other Methods

There are a variety of other ways to clarify the need and define objectives for your survey project: brainstorming, mind mapping, affinity diagrams, and in-depth interviews. A simple, yet effective book that can help you sort through issues and information is David Straker's book, *Rapid Problem Solving With Post-It® Notes* (1997). In that book, Straker presents techniques such as the post-up, swap sort, top-down tree, and others. These techniques are based on research approaches such as affinity diagrams, nominal group, technique, and the KJ method. He presents the approaches in such a way that is useful to those people who were not trained in research methodologies, but need similar tools to address problems and issues.

The point is that when considering a survey project, the first step is to build a foundation for your survey objectives, which will ultimately lead to survey project design as well as specific survey questions. Just like design of a learning and development program is more than simply throwing a few activities together, survey design is more than identifying a need and quickly putting together a list of questions in hopes of gathering useful information. Preliminary work ensures you ask the right questions to the right audience at the right time. It ensures that the survey questions measure what they are intended to measure in order to address a need.

Noted

Building a foundation for your survey objectives will help ensure you ask the right questions at the right time of the right people.

Types of Objectives

Survey objectives can be written one of three ways. They can be written as statements, questions, or hypotheses.

Objectives as Statements

Statements are the classic approach to writing survey objectives. They serve as the basis for descriptive studies more so than experimental studies. As previously mentioned, program objectives serve as evaluation objectives, which, subsequently, represent the survey objective. An example of an objective written as a statement is:

Determine the change in employee engagement for employees in the corporate headquarters one year after the new initiative is completed.

In what ways does this objective inform a survey? First, it indicates that there is a baseline of employee engagement. If the intent is to determine change, a baseline must exist or the objective is unrealistic. This simple statement also indicates what we plan to measure (employee engagement), our population (employees in corporate headquarters), and when we plan to take the measure (one year after the initiative is completed). This particular statement also leads us to consider the research design, a cross-sectional study where we collect data from a particular group at a given point in time. (Research design is discussed in more detail in chapter 3.)

The following objective provides similar information; however, the design of the survey project will be slightly different:

Determine how employee engagement differs one year after the initiative for those who are involved in the program and those who are not involved in the program.

This objective does not necessarily assume there is a baseline on employee engagement. It only suggests that we want to measure employee engagement one year after the initiative. However, this objective targets two groups—participants and nonparticipants of the initiative. So, this one objective tells us that there will be one survey administered to two groups one year after the initiative and the data will be compared between them.

Objectives as Questions

Sometimes we do not know what measures we need to take, or we know the measures but we have no baseline. In these cases our survey objectives may be written as questions rather than statements. For example:

What level of employee engagement exists in our corporate headquarters one year after the initiative?

While indicating there will be a measure of employee engagement for corporate headquarters employees and that the measurement will take place one year after the initiative, this objective also suggests there is no baseline. The intent is to describe the level of employee engagement versus describing a difference in employee engagement.

Objectives written as questions are often the basis for qualitative surveys such as interviews and focus groups. However, they are also used to set the stage for statistical surveys.

Basic Rule

For a given project, you may have multiple objectives. Be consistent in your use of statements, questions, or hypotheses.

Objectives as Hypotheses

Hypotheses as objectives in functions such as learning and development, HR, and meetings and events often reflect specific program objectives. A hypothesis is a specific statement of prediction describing in concrete terms what will happen in your study (Trochim, 2006). Hypotheses are based on previous research or evidence of some perceived truth and imply an experimental research design, even though, more times than not, studies conducted in learning and development, HR, and meetings and events are more descriptive than experimental. Hypotheses are, however, a type of survey objective.

Survey objectives written as hypotheses are written either as a correlational hypothesis or a causal hypothesis. An example of a correlational hypothesis is:

One year after the initiative, employee engagement in the marketing department is 10 percent higher than that of the purchasing department.

This hypothesis indicates that measures of employee engagement will be taken in both the marketing and purchasing departments one year after the initiative. It also assumes prior research has been conducted to theorize that the difference in employee engagement is 10 percent, with marketing being the higher of the two departments. It is a correlational hypothesis because it indicates that the analysis will consider the relationship between the departments and employee engagement scores, but it does not indicate a causal relationship.

A sample of a causal hypothesis is:

Participation in the initiative by employees of the marketing department will lead to a 10 percent increase in employee engagement in that department within one year of participation.

Again, the measures to be taken are those representing employee engagement. The hypothesis assumes there is a basis for the theory that participation in the initiative will lead to an increase in employee engagement within a year of participation. This hypothesis is causal because it implies a cause-and-effect relationship between participation in the initiative and improvement in the employee engagement score.

Think About This

How SMART are your objectives?
Objectives drive survey design and administration. They are also the basis for specific survey questions. The smarter your objectives, the easier it is to obtain useful information from your survey. Check your objectives against the following criteria.

Specific	Objectives must represent specific desired expected outcomes
Measurable	Objectives must be developed so that success is evident. Measurable objectives make it possible to assess whether the intended outcomes are achieved.
Achievable	Objectives must represent achievable results given the conditions, resources, time period, participant ability, and system support.
Relevant	Objectives capture the essence of the goal or purpose and must be tied to the need for the project, initiative, or program.
Time-bound	Objectives must represent the achievement of results within a certain period of time.

*For variations of SMART, visit rapidbi.com/created/WriteSMARTobjectives.html.

Table 2-1 provides additional examples of survey objectives written as statements, questions, and hypotheses. Objectives written as statements are common, particularly for descriptive studies, providing a basic direction for the survey and survey questions. Survey objectives written as questions often lead to qualitative surveys, particularly exploratory studies. In these studies, there is typically no baseline and the intent of the survey is to search for an answer rather than measure a specific phenomenon.

Survey objectives written as hypotheses tend to be more prevalent in experimental and quasi-experimental research projects. Hypotheses assume there is enough research behind the objective to support the theory the objective purports. They read much like the type of statement written as program objectives that drive program evaluation, even though many of these studies are descriptive rather than experimental in nature.

How you write survey objectives is a balance between the purpose of the research project, preference, and organization philosophy and culture. Operationalizing the objectives by defining the specific variables and their attributes will transform a broad objective to the information you need to gather from your survey project.

Basic Rule
Well-written survey objectives are important. But they will serve you little purpose if there is no direct link to the need for the survey. Make sure your survey objectives reflect the defined need.

From Objective to Information

Getting clear on the objectives is the first step toward designing the survey project, which includes writing the survey questions. Before you start writing questions, it is important to identify the specific information needs for each objective. This step operationalizes the objectives so that they are measurable.

Each objective includes one or more variables that represent the measures taken using a survey. Variables are entities that can take on different values. Variables can be quantitative, qualitative, binary (yes/no), composite, or even proxies or indirect measures when it is not feasible to use the real measures. Attributes are the specific values that we place on a variable. They are the way in which we measure a change within the variable. Variables relate to the question stem; attributes relate to response choices. Table 2-2 demonstrates these elements of a survey objective.

Table 2-1. Comparison of Types of Survey Objectives

Objectives as a Statement	Objectives as a Question	Objectives as Hypotheses
Determine administrators' perception of the new learning management system three months after implementation.	What do administrators' think about the new learning management system?	Three months after implementation of the new learning management system, administrators will report 10% less time spent tracking learner participation data than administrators not using the new system.
Determine the perceived change in behavior of first-line supervisors by their supervisors, peers, and direct reports six months after their participation in the program.	How do supervisors, peers, and direct reports perceive their first-line supervisors' leadership behaviors?	Participation in the program by first-line supervisors will lead to at least a 10% increase in employee satisfaction for their departments.
Compare participant ability to apply five steps to managing conflict before participating in the program to ability three months after the program.	Do participants perceive that their ability to apply the five steps to managing conflict have improved since completing the program?	Participation in the conflict management course will result in a 5% improvement in participant ability to apply the five steps to managing conflict six months after participation.
Determine the improvement in net promoter score three months after the program.	What is our current net promoter score?	Three months after the program, net promoter score will be 15% higher for the northwest division than for the southwest division.

Table 2-2. Characteristics of an Objective

If the **objective** is:

Determine the difference in frequency of use of skills taught in the workshop based on tenure within the organization.

The **variables** are:
- Frequency of use
- Tenure

Attributes for each variable may be:

Frequency of use
- Never
- Rarely
- Occasionally
- Frequently
- Very Frequently

Tenure
- Less than 1 year
- 1 to 5 years
- 6 to 10 years
- 11 to 15 years
- 15 to 20 years

General to Specific

Objectives often come to us in broad terms, which is why the tips above are helpful. Through literature review, focus groups, and other means, needs for the survey become clear, which lead to clarity with objectives. But, still, we often contend with moving from broad objectives to a survey instrument, causing us to guess at the appropriate survey questions. When this is the case, simply break down the constructs represented in the objective into specific measurable sub-variables or measures so that useable information can be captured. Below is a simple example.

A survey objective for a conflict management workshop for a midsized nonprofit organization is:

Determine participant reaction to the conflict management workshop.

The variable, "reaction," is quite broad, representing a construct for which we must define specific measures in order to prepare it as the basis for the survey. Reaction can be measured in a variety of ways. Phillips and Phillips (2008) categorize reaction to programs, projects, and initiatives in terms of non-content and content issues. Non-content issues include measures associated with demographics, location, and logistics. Whereas content areas include measures of relevance, importance, and intent to use, as well as those associated with facilitation, timing of the program, and amount of new information.

To make broad objectives such as these more measurable, create an objectives map. Six steps will take you through the objectives map process, which will ultimately lead you to developing SMART objectives.

1. Define broad objective.
2. Identify specific measures (variables).
3. Determine attributes for the measures.
4. Determine the baseline.
5. Set your target.
6. Write your SMART objectives.

Table 2-3 presents these first three steps of the objectives map. Column one presents the broad objective: Determine the reaction of participants to the conflict management workshop upon completion of the workshop. Column two includes the measures of "reaction." Column three lists the attributes that describe the value respondents will place on the different measures. To this point, you are identifying the information you hope to gather through the survey.

Based on the first three steps to developing an objectives map, you can now write your survey objectives as:

1. Determine participant level of agreement that the course content is relevant, useful, and reflective of the real world.
2. Determine the percentage of content expected to use when participants return to the workplace.
3. Determine the most useful tool for participants on the job.
4. Determine participant level of agreement that the facilitator provides complete answers, offers specific examples, anticipates participant needs, and shifts teaching style based on audience dynamics.

5. Determine participant level of agreement that the course is a good use of time and a good use of organization resources.

While you had one broad objective to measure participant reaction to a program, you now have five better-defined objectives that measure the construct. These five objectives provide better guidance to developing your survey given that the variables and their attributes are clearer.

Table 2-3. Partial Objectives Map		
Broad Objective	**Measures**	**Attributes**
Determine participant reaction to the conflict management workshop.	Reaction to:	
	Content Relevance	Content Relevance
	1. Intent to use content	Likert Agreement
	2. Importance to the job	
	3. Reflective of real world	
	4. Content use expectations	Percentages
	5. Usefulness of tools to application on the job (list tools)	Rank Order
	Facilitation	Facilitation
	1. Provides complete answers	Likert Agreement
	2. Offers specific examples	
	3. Anticipates participant needs	
	4. Shifts teaching style based on audience dynamics	
	Overall Satisfaction	Overall Satisfaction
	1. Good use of participant time	Likert Agreement
	2. Good use of organization resources	

Even Better

So what about the last three steps in the objectives map? Completing these steps will make your objectives even better. SMART objectives read much like hypotheses, and for many that is exactly what they are—as long as the theories they purport have enough research to support them. Nevertheless, SMART objectives are the ideal type of objective, regardless of its purpose. SMART objectives give direction to program and project designers, and developers. They guide facilitation and implementation. They serve as the basis for program evaluation, which includes the design and implementation of surveys. SMART objectives also provide guidance in terms of timing of data collection and provide the benchmarks by which to compare survey results. Table 2-4 presents the complete objectives map. Column four presents the baseline data. If available, these data are the basis for setting targets or criterion for results. Column five presents the targets you hope to achieve. Again, these targets are ideally derived from the initial research. Column six lists the SMART objectives. These objectives give clear guidance to the expected outcomes from your survey. They define measures to be taken, timing of data collection, and hoped for results.

Develop good survey objectives and you will improve your chances for delivering a quality survey instrument. Results from the survey will address stakeholder needs. The next chapter will address survey research design.

Think About This

When good objectives are in place, determining the right questions to ask is simple. Refer to Table 2-3. On a piece of paper (or in this book), write the survey questions that measure the survey objectives.

_____

_____

_____

_____

_____

Table 2-4. Complete Objectives Map

Broad Objective	Measures	Attributes	Baseline	Targets	SMART Objectives
Determine participant reaction to the conflict management workshop.	Reaction to: Content Relevance 1. intent to use content 2. importance to the job 3. reflective of real world 4. content use expectations 5. usefulness of tools to application on the job (list tools)	Content Relevance Likert Agreement Percentages Rank Order	Course Relevance 70% of respondents select "Agree" or "Strongly Agree" 60% of respondents select 80% or above No baseline	Course Relevance 80% select "Agree" or "Strongly Agree" 70% select 85% or above Identify most useful tool	Upon completion of the workshop: Course Relevance 80% of respondents "Agree" or "Strongly Agree" that course content is: • relevant • important • reflective of real world 70% of respondents indicate they expect to use at least 85% of the content on the job Respondents rank tools in terms of usefulness
	Facilitation 1. provides complete answers 2. offers specific examples 3. anticipates participant needs 4. shifts teaching style based on audience dynamics	Facilitation Likert Agreement	Facilitation 65% of respondents select "Agree" or "Strongly Agree" on items 1-3 50% of respondents select "Agree" or "Strongly Agree" on item 4; 0 select "Strongly Agree" on item 4	Facilitation 75% select "Agree" or "Strongly Agree" on items 1-3 65% select either "Agree" or "Strongly Agree"	Facilitation 75% of respondents "Agree" or "Strongly Agree" that the facilitator: • provides complete answers • offers specific examples • anticipates participants' needs 65% of respondents "Agree" or "Strongly Agree" that the facilitator: • shifts teaching style based on audience dynamics
	Overall Satisfaction 1. good use of participant time 2. good use of organization resources	Overall Satisfaction Likert Agreement	Overall Satisfaction 65% of respondents select "Agree" or "Strongly Agree" on items 1-2	Overall Satisfaction 75% select "Agree" or "Strongly Agree" on items 1-2	Overall Satisfaction 75% of respondents "Agree" or "Strongly Agree" that the course was a • good use of participant time • good use of organization resources

Noted

Some people will ask if it is necessary to map all objectives to such extreme. The answer is, probably not. However, the more detailed you are up front, the easier it is to develop a survey instrument that delivers useable, relevant information.

Getting It Done

Take a set of objectives, either for a specific survey project, a program, or an evaluation. Compare the objectives to the descriptions above. Are your objectives statements, questions, or do they sound more like hypotheses? Are your objectives SMART? Create an objectives map to help you start drafting your survey questions.

3

Survey Research Design

■ ■

What's Inside This Chapter

In this chapter you will learn the basics of survey research design. After reading this chapter you should be able to

▶ Describe key issues in research design
▶ Explain the difference between experimental and descriptive designs
▶ Determine when and how to sample a population
▶ Plan your survey project

Key Considerations

The survey design guidelines outlined in the previous chapters and throughout this book will help produce a high-quality survey instrument; but to collect useful data, the survey must be administered according to a plan. Research design is an important component of that plan. Guided by the survey objectives, research design further specifies the groups to whom the survey will be administered and the timing of administration, so that results can provide useful information.

Considerations for research design relate to the interpretation of data resulting from the survey. For example, the research design might call for a comparison of one group of people participating in a program, to another group not participating. Comparing the survey results of the two groups determines the influence of the program on performance of the participating group. Research design might also call for the comparison of a group of individuals to itself over time to measure change in some attributes resulting from an intervention. Alternatively, a research design might call for the surveying of one group at one point in time to determine group members' perceptions of some phenomenon. One of the most fundamental objectives of survey research design is to ensure that the study correctly answers the questions it addresses with the data it collects, an achievement referred to as internal validity (Swanson and Holton, 2005).

Internal Validity

Internal validity refers to the validity of inferences made from a study. Internal validity shows how well a study was run in terms of design, measures taken, and measures not taken. The amount of confidence a researcher has in inferring a causal relationship between an event and an outcome is determined by internal validity. Its relevance lies more in experimental studies than descriptive studies. For example, a large retail store chain implemented an interactive selling skills program to help improve sales. Salespeople from three stores received the training. Sales occurring three months after the program were compared to sales of three similar stores not participating in the training. The difference in store sales between the participating group and the non-participating group was significant. Internal validity tells us how well the design of this study controlled for other influencing factors that could also affect sales.

Along with internal validity, another key issue in research design is external validity. External validity refers to the extent to which results from the study can be generalized to a larger population.

External Validity

While internal validity concerns the quality of the design and truth in conclusions, external validity concerns the extent to which this truth exists with other groups, people, or situations. Essentially, external validity concerns the reliability with which findings are repeatable. Trochim (2006) suggests that there are two approaches that can be used to provide evidence that results can be generalized: the sampling model approach, and the proximal similarity model.

Noted

Campbell and Stanley (1966) identified eight factors that can jeopardize a study's internal validity.

1. **History**: refers to the effect external events have on subjects between the various measurements taken during an experiment.

2. **Maturation**: refers to how subjects naturally change over time (rather than due to the program of process under evaluation).

3. **Testing**: refers to how a pretest can affect a respondent's performance on a post-test. Pretesting often results in contamination of the respondent's performance or selection in response choices.

4. **Instrumentation**: refers to the objectivity, reliability, and validity of the research instrument and measurements. Biased or unreliable data can threaten a study's internal validity, as can changing the measurement methods.

5. **Statistical Regression**: exists when retest results regress toward the mean. For example, when participants are selected for a program because they test high on the pretest, the group's average score on the retest tend to be lower. The same happens when participants are selected for a program because test scores are lower than average. Retest results tend to be higher.

6. **Selection**: refers to the effect of comparing groups that are not equivalent in terms of factors that can influence outcomes. Controlling for differences by matching the two groups prior to the study will reduce the risks that observed differences in outcomes between the groups is due to differences in the groups rather than the program or intervention.

7. **Experimental Mortality/Attrition**: refers to the potential bias that occurs when participants of the study drop out, altering the makeup of the groups.

8. **Selection Interactions**: refers to effect selection method has on maturation, history, or instrumentation.

The sampling model approach begins with identifying the population for which you would like to generalize results, then, draw an appropriate sample from that population. (Sampling is covered later in the chapter). Because your sample is representative of the population, you can generalize back to it. Unfortunately, it is not always possible to use this method. First, you may not have a clear definition of your population. Second, you may be unable to collect data from a large enough or representative enough sample. Third, you may not be able to collect data at different time frames in order to capture a true sample.

The second approach Trochim suggests is the proximal similarity model (Campbell, 1963). In applying this approach, the researcher identifies the different people, places, and time that are more or less similar to those in the study and the likelihood these factors would alter the research results. Placing different contexts on their relative similarities allows you to develop a "proximal similarity framework" or "gradient of similarity" that you can use as the basis for generalizing findings.

Basic Rule

According to Trochim (2006) with the proximal similarity model, you can never generalize with certainty—it is always a question of more or less similar.

Noted

Campbell and Stanley (1966) and Issac and Michael (1971) cite four factors that can adversely affect a study's external validity.

1. **Selection Interaction:** As in the case of internal validity, sample selection can influence a study's results. If a sample of people is randomly drawn, this might influence the performance of those individuals, thereby influencing outcomes of the study.

2. **Pretesting:** Pretesting may influence participants' behavior and response to a program or treatment. Given that the population did not undergo the same pretest, this would make the sample group dissimilar from the population, thereby affecting the researcher's ability to generalize.

3. **Setting:** Response or performance of participants is often the result of being a part of a study. For example, observation can often influence performance, negating the impact of the program under study. Known as the Hawthorne Effect, the setting itself becomes an influencing factor and makes the sample group one factor less similar from the population, reducing the accuracy with which we can infer general results.

4. **Multiple Treatments/Interventions:** Involvement in multiple programs or interventions can have a cumulative effect on results. If a person participates in one program, then later participates in another, the effect of the first program still exists. Unless the population participated in the first program as well, the program is an unaccounted for difference in the sample and population.

Research Designs

There are a variety of types of research designs; which one you choose depends on the purpose and objectives of your survey project. Broad classifications of research designs are experimental designs and descriptive designs, also referred to as observational studies. One fundamental difference between the two is the manipulation of program, event, or intervention under investigation by the researcher. With experimental research design, the researcher manipulates the independent variable or "treatment" to observe its effects on some outcome. The researcher will interject a program or intervention and randomly assign participants to two groups: one group participates in the program and the other group does not. By comparing results of the experiment, researchers can make assumptions about the cause-and-effect relationship between the program (or "treatment") and the observed outcomes. Descriptive designs can also show comparisons between groups, but the "treatment" already exists. This means that the researcher is not interjecting a program or initiative; rather, she is asking relevant questions about a particular program or initiative that has already occurred. Through analysis, the researcher determines whether or not an association exists between various factors and the program. However, results from descriptive studies do not describe a causal relationship.

Here is a simple example. Your preliminary research shows that few employees participate in a routine exercise program. It also shows that the number of doctor visits by employees continues to increase. Executives want to offer employees gym memberships to help reduce their doctor visits; however, they first want to know if routine exercise will be effective in reducing these visits. In an effort to determine whether or not routine exercise will reduce doctor visits, you decide to conduct a study. The broad research objective is: *Determine the relationship between the number of doctor visits by employees who exercise routinely and those who do not.*

To determine if routine exercise causes a reduction in doctor visits, you would use an experimental design (all ethical issues aside). You would randomly assign a sample of the target population to two groups. One group, the experimental group, receives access to the gym along with a prescribed exercise routine. The second group, the control group, receives nothing. After a designated period of time, you compare the average number of doctor visits between the two groups to determine if there is a significant difference. Using this design, the researcher interjects the treatment, which is the gym membership and exercise routine, then assigns participants and nonparticipants.

On the other hand, you can also make a comparison between two groups using descriptive design. To do so, survey employees about their exercise routines and the average number of times they visit the doctor. Through data analysis, you would determine if there is an association between exercise and number of doctor visits. In this scenario, the researcher is not interjecting a "treatment." The "treatment," which is routine exercise, already exists for those who respond that they partake in it.

Basic Rule
When trying to choose the best research design consider purpose, objectives, context, time, and resources.

Within each of the broad research design classification are specific designs. The remainder of this section describes a few of the designs that may be useful in your survey project.

Experimental Designs

Experimental designs include surveys that can be taken before, during, and after a program, event, or intervention. They compare results between two groups of randomly selected participants. True experimental designs require the random assignment of participants to either the experimental or control group. However, there are other designs that take on similar characteristics of the true experimental design. Fink (2003b) identifies five types of experimental designs:

- randomized concurrent controls
- non-randomized concurrent controls
- self-controls
- historical controls
- combination designs.

Randomized Concurrent Control

Randomized concurrent control is the classic experimental design and depicts a true experiment. The first step is to randomly assign participants to an experimental group or control group. Then take pre-program measures from both groups. Interject the program or intervention, then, at a designated point in time, take post-program measures. In this design you are looking for a change in the pre- and post-measures for each group, and comparing the change in performance between the two groups. This classic experimental design (shown in Figure 3-1) answers the question: *What is the difference in the change in performance between the two groups?*

Figure 3-1. Classic Design

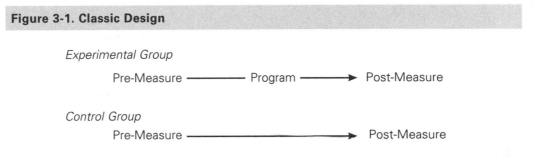

Post-program only design is the simplest of the randomized concurrent control because it only involves the post-program measures. Figure 3-2 shows this design. Using this approach, randomly select the two groups. Note: To control for performance in your outcome data, the population from which you draw the sample must be performing at the same level. Intervene with a program, then at a predetermined time after the intervention, capture the post-program data and compare results between the two groups. In this design, you are answering the question: *What is the difference in performance between the two groups?*

Figure 3-2. Post-Program Only Design

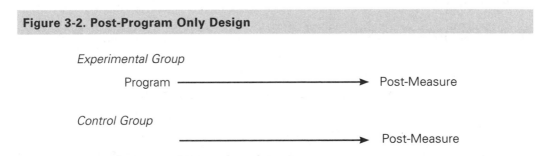

The ideal randomized concurrent control design is known as Solomon Four Group Design. Solomon Four Group Design is a combination of the classic and post-program only designs. There are two pretests, two experimental groups, and two controls groups, randomly selected. Solomon Four Group Design controls for nearly all types of invalidity. This approach, shown in Figure 3-3, reduces the influence of other factors that may affect performance in the measures of interest, including the effects of the pretest. While Solomon Four Group Design answers multiple questions, a fundamental question it answers is: *Is the difference in performance due to the test?*

Figure 3-3. Solomon Four Group Design

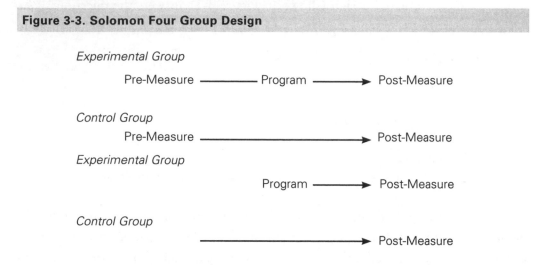

Solomon Four Group Design is robust, yet it is expensive and comprehensive and not routinely used in organizational settings. An alternative design that drops out the second control group may be more appropriate, yet, it also adds to the cost of your project. In this design, there is only one pretest and one control group, but there are two experimental groups. Figure 3-4 shows this alternative to Solomon Four Group Design.

Figure 3-4. Alternative Design

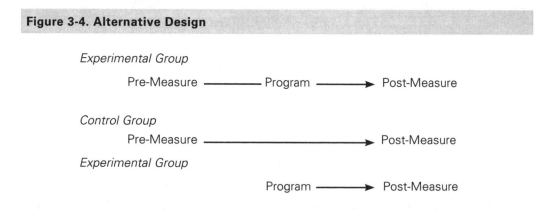

Non-Randomized Concurrent Controls

Also referred to as quasi-experimental design, nonequivalent controls, and nonrandomized control trials, nonrandom concurrent control designs compare two groups that have not been randomly selected. This design is most often seen in organization settings with limited opportunity to randomly select participants and nonparticipants of a program. The actual designs are similar to those shown in the previous figures. The key difference is the randomization.

For example, a large telecommunications company wants to pilot test a new sales training program for its retail stores and the program's impact on weekly sales per employee. They select participants based on current sales, types of products sold, and tenure with the company. Three months after the program, weekly sales of the participating group will be compared to weekly sales of a similar, nonparticipating group. In this example, participants were chosen for the participant and nonparticipating groups using a set of criteria, but they were not randomly assigned to each group.

Think About This

Federal Information Agency

A large U.S. federal government agency had unusually higher turnover in a 1500-employee job family, their technical specialists. Turnover was approximately 38 percent. The preliminary research found that the cause of the turnover was pay. The agency, by law, is required to cap pay at a certain level for various job families. So there was nothing they could do to resolve the root cause of the turnover problem. However, the analysis also showed there was interest by the employee group in upskilling their technical expertise, specifically through a graduate program where an advanced degree could be obtained.

The agency partnered with a local university to pilot the master's degree. The program took three years to complete and included, rather than a thesis, a project that would add value back to the agency in terms of efficiency gains. The school could only accommodate 100 students at a time.

Candidates for the program were selected based on the following criteria:

- A candidate should have at least one year of service prior to beginning classes.

- A candidate must meet the normal requirements to be accepted into the graduate school at the university.

- A candidate must be willing to sign a commitment to stay with the agency for two years beyond program completion.

- A candidate's immediate manager must nominate the employee for consideration.

- A candidate must be considered "high potential" as rated by the immediate manager.

The agency decided to move forward with the pilot, but wanted to evaluate its success on reducing turnover as well as the contribution of the course projects to selected 100 participants for the pilot. A nonrandomized control group arrangement was applied to determine if the outcome (reduced turnover) was actually due to the master's degree program. The experimental group was made up of the 100 participants in the pilot. The control group was made up of another 100 employees from the 1500-employee population who met the program criteria. The two groups were tracked for four years. Below is the comparison of turnover between the two groups:

Annualized Avoidable Turnover	1 Year Prior to Program	1st Year Sept. to Aug.	2nd Year Sept. to Aug.	3rd Year Sept. to Aug.	1 Year Post-Program
Total Group (1,500)	38%	39%	36%	35%	34%
Program Participants Group (100)	N/A	5% (5)	4% (4)	3% (3)	3% (3)
Similar Group (100)	N/A	34%	35%	33%	36%
Four-Year Expected Turnover Statistics = 138					
Four-Year Actual Turnover Statistics = 15					
Four-Year Total Group Turnover Statistics = 144 (with a base of 100)					

Source: Phillips, P.P. and Phillips, J.J. (editors). (2010). Master's Degree Program: Federal Information Agency. In *Proving the Value of HR, 2nd edition.* Birmingham, AL: ROI Institute, Inc.

As you can see in the table, there is a significant difference in turnover between the two groups.

Question to Think About:

Of the eight threats to internal validity identified by Campbell and Stanley, which one threat is most obvious in this case study?

Go to Appendix A: Answers to *Think About This* Exercises for the answer.

Self Controls

Comparing participants' pre/post responses is a classic research design, particularly in the learning and development, HR, and meetings and events areas. In this case, the individual respondent serves as the control group and the experimental group. Prior to a program, the participant performance has not been influenced by a program or intervention. Once a program is put into place, this new influence affects the individual's performance. A typical example of this design is the pre/post learning assessment. Prior to a program, participants respond to a survey or test to measure their knowledge in certain skill areas. They then participate in a program intended to improve those skill areas. The program is the "treatment." Post-program participants respond to a second survey or test after the program to measure their knowledge in the skill areas.

Another example of self-controls design is interrupted time series. Interrupted time series analysis is used to determine whether an outside event such as a program or process affected subsequent observations of measures in question. The measures are observed multiple times before the program and after the program as shown in Figure 3-5.

Figure 3-5. Interrupted Time Series

$$O_1 \quad O_2 \quad O_3 \quad O_4 \quad O_5 \quad \text{Program} \quad O_6 \quad O_7 \quad O_8 \quad O_9 \quad O_{10}$$

Historical Controls

Historical control studies compare data from individuals who have been followed in the past, or for whom data have already been recorded, to individuals who are currently participating in a program, event, or intervention. A classic example is the norm-reference test. Success with the test is compared to the scores of all individuals who have participated in the past. Another example of historical control may be the success of a new onboarding program intended to help new employees get up-to-speed so they can produce at a certain level within a certain timeframe. New hires have no baseline for measuring improved performance, so their performance may be compared to that of previous new hires.

Combination Designs

Occasionally, there is opportunity to combine designs in order to achieve a survey project's purpose. Just as the name infers, combination designs bring together multiple designs in an effort to take the best measurements. For example, if you are interested in measuring the change in trend data for a group of participants after they participate in a program, but you are also interested in knowing how much that program influenced the change in trend data, you could combine time series analysis with concurrent control. This multiple-time series design measures the change in performance at different intervals for each group, and determines if a greater difference occurs as a result of a program or event. Figure 3-6 shows multiple-time series.

Figure 3-6. Multiple-Time Series

Experimental Group

O_1 O_2 O_3 O_4 O_5 Program O_6 O_7 O_8 O_9 O_{10}

Control Group

O_1 O_2 O_3 O_4 O_5 ———— O_6 O_7 O_8 O_9 O_{10}

Noted

A scientific or technical study always consists of the following three steps:
1. Decide the objective.
2. Consider the method.
3. Evaluate the method in relation to the objective.
—Gen'ichi Taguchi, Japanese engineer and statistician

Descriptive Designs

As previously mentioned, descriptive studies are different from experimental designs in a variety of ways. One specific difference is the researcher's role in the process. With experimental designs, the researcher interjects a program, event, or intervention of some sort and observes the outcome as a result. With descriptive designs, the "treatment," if one exists, has already occurred and associations rather than causal relationships are examined. But sometimes, a descriptive study is merely a look into the status of a given situation using a survey as a means to do so. There are several types of descriptive studies. Three specific types relevant to learning and development, HR, and meetings and events are:

▸ cross-sectional designs

▸ cohort designs

▸ case-control designs.

Cross-Sectional Designs

Application of cross-sectional survey design is common within and outside organizations. Through the use of cross-sectional design, you simply gather data from a target audience at a given point in time. For example, you may want to survey your employees to assess their perception of the learning function. You administer a survey one time to gather these data. This is a cross-sectional survey. In essence you have taken a cross-section of a measure of their perception; whereas, with a longitudinal study, such as time-series studies, measurements are taken at multiple times over a period of time.

Noted

Definitions of longitudinal studies vary. According to Trochim (2006) there are two types of longitudinal studies: repeated measures and time series. If you take two or a few measurements, you have repeated measures. If you take at least 20 measures over a period of time, you have time series.

Cohort Designs

A cohort is a group of individuals who share a common trait or experience. Cohort studies, a type of longitudinal study, focus on that group and track it over time. In some cohort studies, the members of the sample group may change, even though all participants in the sample are part of the larger cohort. For example, you might want to survey participants of your organization's health and wellness program to measure their attitude toward exercise and its effect on their productivity at work. There are 2,000 participants who began the program in 2010. You might survey a random sample of participants in 2010, then another random sample in 2011, and still another in 2012. While respondents in your sample groups may be entirely different for each survey, they are all participants of the 2010 health and wellness cohort.

Panel designs are a type of cohort design (Fink, 2003b) in that they are longitudinal studies and track a cohort over time. The differentiating characteristic of a panel is that panel studies track the same sample over time—meaning the members of the sample group do not change. Using the health and wellness program as an example, rather than randomly selecting a new sample each year, you measure participant attitude toward exercise, with a panel study. You will select your sample group and administer the survey to that same group in 2010, 2011, and 2012.

Cohort studies can be conducted prospectively or retrospectively. Prospective studies require the collection of new data from members of the cohort. Retrospective studies use the same approach, but the study is performed post hoc. You can use as many years of existing data as you need and have available, but the time to complete a retrospective study is much less than a prospective study.

Case Control Designs

Case control studies are retrospective studies comparing a group of individuals who differ in the outcome of interest. The purpose of such studies is often to identify a cause for this difference. For example, from an employee population of 10,000, you divide the group based on those who have reported at least five doctor visits in a 12-month period and those who have reported fewer than five. Using stratified random sampling (described in more detail in the next section), you randomly select 100 from each group. You then administer a survey to members of each group asking them to report on factors that could influence the number of visits to the doctor, such as:

- ▸ exercise routine
- ▸ gym membership
- ▸ smoking habits
- ▸ eating habits
- ▸ stress on the job
- ▸ satisfaction with work.

Through data analysis you discover which factors have the strongest association with number of visits to the doctor.

Sampling

Applying the best design given the purpose and objectives of your survey project, along with time and resource constraints, will ensure you report reliable, useful information. Sampling is part of that design. Sampling ensures that the right people and the right number of people provide useable data so that inference can be made to a larger population. Note that sampling is not appropriate for all survey projects. It is a process through which we collect data from a smaller number of respondents than the number of people in our population. For many survey projects, the population is so small that there is no need to sample or the project is not suitable for sampling. This is often true in program evaluation when the purpose of the survey is to describe the success of a program. Also, when conducting purely qualitative studies, statistical sampling is inappropriate.

The main reason for sampling is economy. Sampling was devised centuries ago when researchers set out to poll the population through means that were less convenient than those today. At the time, statisticians, psychometricians, and researchers agreed that the cost of administering one more survey was greater than the value of the data from that survey. So, they devised a technique through which we can determine the most appropriate number of people from whom we should collect data, given the size of the population. Technology has eased the cost of surveying and makes it much more convenient for most organization projects. However, sampling is an important tool for many survey projects.

Sampling Process

Sample selection begins with the population selection. The population is the group of individuals or entities we are interested in studying. It is the group that holds the information we are seeking through our survey project. When identifying the population, it is important not to confuse the theoretical population and the study population. The theoretical population is the universe of those who hold the information in which you are interested, but you do not necessarily have access to them. Because access is not always available, you focus on the population to which you do have access. It is the accessible population from whom we will draw the sample. Differentiation between the theoretical population and the accessible population is more relevant to large-scale social science survey projects than to typical organization-wide survey projects, but is an important difference with which many people working on their first major survey project tend to struggle.

A few guidelines to help you identify the population include:

▶ Ensure the population consists of those people who actually possess the information sought by the survey.

▶ Identify all major factors that would otherwise qualify respondents and make their response meaningful to stakeholders.

▶ Define specific criteria for inclusion and exclusion of respondents.

▶ Ensure the population you are targeting is accessible.

The sample is a subset of the population. The sample must hold the same characteristics as the population; otherwise, you cannot infer results from the smaller to the larger group. Figure 3-7 depicts the relationship between the population and the sample.

Figure 3-7. Relationship Between Population and Sample

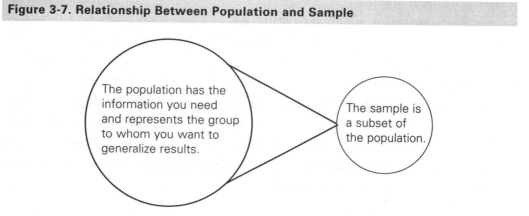

The population has the information you need and represents the group to whom you want to generalize results.

The sample is a subset of the population.

The sampling frame is the list from which the sample is drawn. Sampling units are the smallest unit that will provide one response—this is typically an individual, but could also be a business unit, department, or a widget from an assembly line if you are surveying widgets for quality defects, for example.

To help clarify the progression from population to sampling unit, here is a simple example. Suppose you are interested in knowing best practices of learning and development managers when it comes to using data for decision-making. Your theoretical population includes all learning and development managers. Because you cannot access every learning and development manager worldwide, you narrow your focus to learning and development managers who are accessible.

Given your relationship with ASTD and the various chapters, you know that learning and development managers who are members are accessible; therefore, you refine the purpose of your study to be: *Describe best practices in data use for decision making from the perspective of learning and development managers who are members of ASTD.* Members of your population are learning managers who are members of ASTD, both national and local chapters. The sample will be a subset of this population; and the sampling frame will be the member lists from ASTD's various chapters. The sampling unit will be the learning and development manager. Figure 3-8 summarizes this connection between population and sampling unit.

Figure 3-8. From Population to Sampling Unit

Purpose of the Study: To describe best practices in data use for decision making from the perspective of learning and development managers who are members of ASTD.

Population	Learning and development managers who are members of ASTD
Sample	Subset of these managers
Sampling Frame	ASTD national and chapter member lists
Sampling Unit	Learning and development manager

To select the sample, you will use one of the following sample selection methods.

Sample Selection Methods

There are a variety of types of sampling techniques. Census, while described below, is not a sampling technique. It is a process of collecting data from the entire populations. Common sampling techniques include:

- ▶ census
- ▶ simple random sampling
- ▶ stratified random sampling
- ▶ systematic random sampling
- ▶ simple cluster sampling
- ▶ multi-stage sampling
- ▶ convenience sampling.

government
& research — *would, PP would*
take to long to get
wouldn't be practical

Census

A census is simply a survey of the entire population. A census is conducted when it is important to hear from everyone in the defined group. We in the United States recognize census from the population survey taken every 10 years. Other types of census are employee surveys conducted in large organizations when it is important to hear from everyone in the company. Sometimes it is impossible for us to reach every person. Cost to do so may be too high, convenience may prevent us from doing so, or the survey project itself does not require it. For example, in a program evaluation, 1,000 employees may ultimately participate, but the population under study is the 100 involved in the pilot program. Because we need input from all participants, we are, in essence, taking a census when we administer the survey.

An example where a census is not as feasible, however, is in the evaluation of a large conference. For example, if we wanted to evaluate the ASTD International Conference & Exposition, it would be almost impossible to capture data from everyone attending the conference resources; time and convenience (or lack thereof) would prevent us from doing so. So, to get a reasonably good measure of the opinions of all conference participants, we would use one of the sample selection methods described next.

Simple Random Sample

Simple random sampling is one of the most commonly used approaches to sample selection and one with which most people are familiar. A simple random sample requires that the entire population be accessible. Sampling units are selected randomly; however, every person in the group has equal opportunity to be selected.

There are a variety of ways to identify a sample through simple random selection. The classic approach to simple random sampling from a relatively small population is through the use of a random number table. Table 3-1 presents an example of a random numbers table.

A random numbers table is a computer-generated table of random numbers. By identifying the members of the population, or your sample units, and listing then numbering them, you can identify the number and select your positional respondents on a random basis. An example follows.

You have 100 supervisors in your organization. You want to select 10 supervisors to serve as a sample for a study underway. List the supervisors 00 through 99; then, using the random numbers table shown in Table 3-1, select the first 10 supervisors by working your way across the top row. You should find that the following supervisors are identified as your participants in the sample.

▸ Supervisor #51

▸ Supervisor #77

▸ Supervisor #27

▸ Supervisor #46

▸ Supervisor #40

▸ Supervisor #42

▸ Supervisor #33

- ▶ Supervisor #12
- ▶ Supervisor #90
- ▶ Supervisor #44
- ▶ Supervisor #46

Table 3-1. Random Numbers Table

Random Number Table

51772	74640	42331	29044	46621	62898	93582	04186	19640	87056
24033	23491	83587	06568	21960	21387	76105	10863	97453	90581
45939	60173	52078	25424	11645	55870	56974	37428	93507	94271
30586	02133	75797	45406	31041	86707	12973	17169	88116	42187
03585	79353	81938	82322	96799	85659	36081	50884	14070	74950
64937	03355	95863	20790	65304	55189	00745	65253	11822	15804
15630	64759	51135	98527	62586	41889	25439	88036	24034	67283
09448	56301	57683	30277	94623	85418	68829	06652	41982	49159
21631	91157	77331	60710	52290	16835	48653	71590	16159	14676
91097	17480	29414	06829	87843	28195	27279	47152	35683	47280
50532	25496	95652	42457	73547	76552	50020	24819	52984	76168
07136	40876	79971	54195	25708	51817	36732	72484	94923	75936
27989	64728	10744	08396	56242	90985	28868	99431	50995	20507
85184	73949	36601	46253	00477	25234	09908	36574	72139	70185
54398	21154	97810	36764	32869	11785	55261	59009	38714	38723
65544	34371	09591	07839	58892	92843	72828	91341	84821	63886
08263	65952	85762	64236	39238	18776	84303	99247	46149	03229
39817	67906	48236	16057	81812	15815	63700	85915	19219	45943
62257	14077	79443	95203	02479	30763	92486	54083	23631	05825
53298	90276	62545	21944	16530	03878	07516	95715	02526	33537

Source: Spiegel, M.R. (1961). *Theory and Problems of Statistics*. New York: McGraw-Hill.

These supervisors will participate in your sample. The random numbers table is suitable for smaller populations from which you will identify a sample. For larger populations, you might choose to use a random numbers generator, which is a simpler approach to randomly selecting your sample. A free and easy-to-use random numbers generator can be found at www.graphpad.com.

1. Go to www.graphpad.com.
2. Select "GraphPad QUICKCALCS."
3. Select "Random Numbers."

4. Select "Continue."
5. Select "Randomly select a subset of subjects."
6. Select "Continue."
7. Input the number of subjects you'd like to randomly select from your population in the first response space and put the number of people in your population in the second response space. You can repeat for as many groups as you need.
8. The output will give you a list of random numbers selected from your population numbers. The population will then be matched to the corresponding names in your sampling frame.

Using the random numbers generator offered through GraphPad and other available resources makes simple random sampling simple.

Stratified Random Sampling

Stratified random sampling is another useful sampling method for survey research. Stratified random sampling simply means that you will randomly select your sample from a given strata in which the respondents are categorized. A stratum is a simple categorization or group identified based on some important demographic or other characteristic. For example, you may be interested in conducting a midyear employee satisfaction survey. While this survey does not take the place of the annual census of employees, it does provide you with a midyear check to see how your employees are faring given recent changes in the organization. Your organization spans the continental United States and is managed by region, so your strata are the regions in which employees work. You then randomly select a sample of employees from each region.

Systematic Random Sampling

Systematic random sampling is simply the process of identifying potential participants of your survey using a systematic approach such as every seventh employee. This is different from simple random sampling in that everyone does not have an equal chance of being picked. Every seventh person is the identified participant. How do you determine if it is to be every seventh person versus every 10th? It's really quite simple. Consider the number of people in your population; divide it by the number of surveys you need to administer to get your target sample size (sample size divided by estimated response rate). For example, suppose your population includes 1,000 people. You want a sample size of 277. You estimate a 50 percent response rate. Therefore, you need 554 respondents identified in your sample (277/.50=554).

Divide 1,000 by 554 and it should result in 1.8. This tells you to select every 2nd person within your population to apply systematic sampling.

Simple Cluster Sample

Simple cluster sampling is similar to stratified random sampling; however, the cluster or group is less strategically defined than in the stratified random sampling. A cluster is a convenient group where your potential respondents reside. For example, a cluster may be a department, team, or committee.

Multi-Stage Sampling

Multi-stage sampling is a series of simple random samples taken at different stages. It helps reduce the time and expense of random sampling from a large area. This technique of sampling is most relevant to surveys that cover a population across a large geographic area and for which data are collected on site, such as household surveys. In multi-stage sampling, a large geographic area is reduced to smaller geographic regions. A random selection of these smaller regions is taken. In the next stage, these regions are divided into even smaller regions and from this group, another random sample is taken. This process continues until the appropriate sampling units are identified.

Convenience Sampling

Convenience sampling is just as it sounds—convenient. Convenient sampling requires no strategy, no statistics, and no calculations. A convenient sample is a group that is convenient. For example, if you want to survey a large operation but the senior executive does not want you to disturb the entire department, he may identify three groups to whom you can administer your survey. This is convenient. Or, if you want to interview participants of a leadership development program and rather than randomly selecting potential interviewees, you ask for volunteers, this represents a convenient sample. Convenience sampling is easy and inexpensive. It is useful in surveying pilot groups or studying relationships between different phenomena. But, it also has some inherent flaws. For example, convenience samples typically are not representative of the larger population of interest, thereby limiting the researcher's ability to generalize findings.

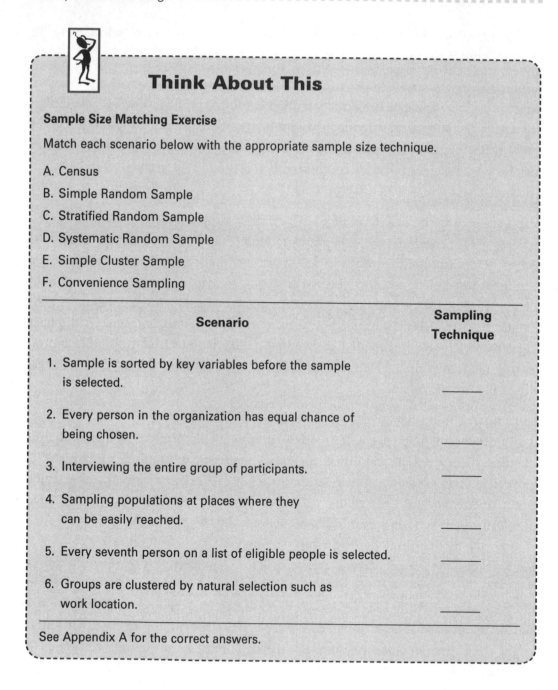

Think About This

Sample Size Matching Exercise

Match each scenario below with the appropriate sample size technique.

A. Census

B. Simple Random Sample

C. Stratified Random Sample

D. Systematic Random Sample

E. Simple Cluster Sample

F. Convenience Sampling

Scenario	Sampling Technique
1. Sample is sorted by key variables before the sample is selected.	_____
2. Every person in the organization has equal chance of being chosen.	_____
3. Interviewing the entire group of participants.	_____
4. Sampling populations at places where they can be easily reached.	_____
5. Every seventh person on a list of eligible people is selected.	_____
6. Groups are clustered by natural selection such as work location.	_____

See Appendix A for the correct answers.

Sample Size Considerations

One of the most frequently asked questions when discussing sampling is, "What is the appropriate sample size for my study?" The answer to this question is, "It depends." Calculating sample size is not as straightforward as some would like to believe.

Dillman, Smyth, and Christian (2009) identify four considerations when determining sample size:

- ▶ the size of the population
- ▶ the homogeneity of the population
- ▶ the margin of error you're willing to accept (confidence interval)
- ▶ the desired confidence level that the results represent the population.

The population size is the number of units (people, organizations, businesses) who hold the information in which you are interested. As the size of the population increases, the number of units required in your sample decreases as a proportion of that population.

Homogeneity refers to "likeness" of the group. Basically, the concern here is the likelihood that respondents will answer the survey questions the same way. Diversity of group members (gender, race, organization tenure, department, and so on) as well as the variance in response choices are considerations when determining homogeneity. If the question is binominal (yes/no), there is a 50 percent probability that one or the other answer will be selected. If a five-point Likert scale is used, there is less probability that respondents will answer each item the same way. The more alike a group is in terms of demographic information and response choice, the fewer people you need in your sample. The more diverse the group and response choice, the more people you need in your sample.

Confidence interval is the range of results you can expect from your population as compared to the results of your survey given the specified margin of error. The margin of error describes the acceptable difference between the true population results and the sample results. For example, if you accept a margin of error of +/– 4 percent and 47 percent of your sample picks an answer, your results suggest the true result lies between 43 percent (47 – 4) and 51 percent (47 + 4). Convention suggests +/– 5 percent margin of error is acceptable; however, an acceptable margin of error is relative to the risk associated with making a wrong decision based on survey results. The less error you need in your results, the more people you need in your sample.

shou *accurate* *attained*
signif *confid*

Confidence level tells you how certain you can be that the results from your sample represent the population within the set margin of error. For example, if you identify 95 percent confidence level and a margin of error of +/– 4 percent and your results show that 47 percent of respondents select an answer, you are reporting that you are 95 percent certain that 47 percent of the actual population would select the same response within a margin of error of +/– 4 percent. Or, another way to put it is that you are 95 percent confident that 43 percent to 51 percent of the population would select the same response. The more confident you want to be in your response, the more people you need in your sample. Table 3-2 summarizes these considerations when determining sample size.

Table 3-2. Considerations When Determining Sample Size	
Population size	The larger the population the more people you need in your sample, although, sample size does not grow proportionately with population size.
Homogeneity of the group	If the group is alike and there is little variance in response choice, you can sample fewer people. If the group is alike and there is variance in the response choice, you need to sample more people. If the group is diverse and there is variance in the response choice, you need to sample even more people.
Margin of error	If you can tolerate error, you can sample fewer people. If you can tolerate little to no error, you need to sample more people.
Confidence level	If you need to be only slightly confident that results represent the population within the stated margin of error, you can sample fewer people. If you need to be certain that results represent the population within the stated margin of error, you need to sample more people.

Sample Size Calculation

There are three ways to calculate the sample size when your survey project warrants it:

- ▶ formulas
- ▶ sample size calculator
- ▶ sample size chart.

Formulas

Multiple formulas exist to help you calculate sample size. There are the more complicated formulas for which much research has been conducted as foundation for their development. But there are also less complicated formulas that sometimes provide a "good enough" estimate.

Noted

"Good enough" is defined, in part, by the risk you are willing to take that your results lead you and stakeholders to a wrong decision and the consequence of that wrong decision.

Two formulas that can help you calculate an appropriate sample size are as follows. First, the more complicated formula:

$$N_s = \frac{(N_p)(p)(1-p)}{(Np-1)(B/C)2 + (p)(1-p)}$$

Where:

- ▶ N_s = the completed sample size needed for the desired level of precision.
- ▶ N_p = the size of the population.
- ▶ p = the proportion of the population expected to choose one of the two response categories.
- ▶ B = margin of error.
- ▶ C = Z-score* associated with the confidence level (1.96 corresponds to the 95 percent confidence level).

*The z-score is a standardized score, given the mean and the standard deviation. Convention assumes 95 percent confidence level; in this case, your z-score will be 1.96.

This formula assumes a binomial response choice (yes/no) and considers factors covered in the previous section. You can find this formula in Dillman, Smyth, and Christian (2003).

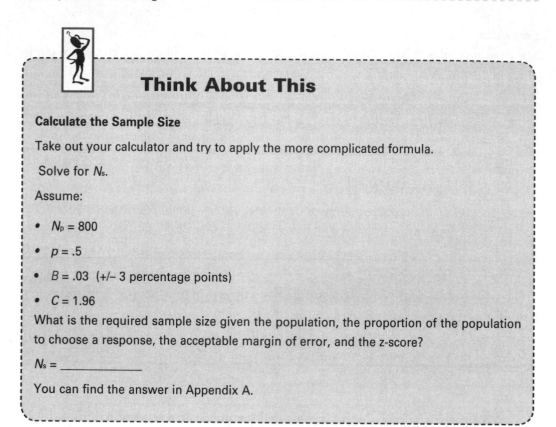

Think About This

Calculate the Sample Size

Take out your calculator and try to apply the more complicated formula.

Solve for N_s.

Assume:

- $N_p = 800$
- $p = .5$
- $B = .03$ (+/– 3 percentage points)
- $C = 1.96$

What is the required sample size given the population, the proportion of the population to choose a response, the acceptable margin of error, and the z-score?

$N_s =$ _____

You can find the answer in Appendix A.

An even simpler approach is to calculate the sample size based on acceptable margin of error. Just divide one by the margin of error squared and you should have a reasonable number for your sample. The formula is:

$$N_s = \frac{1}{\text{error}^2} \cdot \frac{1}{s^2}$$

With an acceptable margin of error of .05, your sample size would be 400.

Sample Size Calculators

To make sample size calculations even easier, a variety of sample size calculators are now available. One such calculator is published by Raosoft available at: www.raosoft.com/samplesize.html. Provide the following information and the sample size is calculated:

- ▶ margin of error
- ▶ confidence level

▶ population

▶ response distribution (proportion responses—they suggest leaving it at 50 percent).

Sample Size Chart

The simplest approach to calculating sample size is with the use of a sample size chart. Table 3-3 is a sample size table for proportions. This table is useful if you are interested in calculating a sample for which you are 95 percent confident that population results will fall within a margin of error of +/− 5 percent and your response choices are binomial (yes/no).

Table 3-3. A Sample Size Table for Proportions

Pop.	Sam.	Pop.	Sam.	Pop.	Sam.	Pop.	Sam.	Pop.	Sam.	Pop.	Sam.
10	9	90	73	230	144	480	213	1400	301	6000	361
15	14	95	76	240	147	500	217	1500	305	7000	364
20	19	100	79	250	151	550	226	1600	309	8000	366
25	23	110	85	260	155	600	234	1700	313	9000	368
30	27	120	91	270	158	650	241	1800	316	10000	369
35	32	130	97	280	162	700	248	1900	319	15000	374
40	36	140	102	290	165	750	254	2000	322	20000	376
45	40	150	108	300	168	800	259	2200	327	30000	379
50	44	160	113	320	174	850	264	2400	331	40000	380
55	48	170	118	340	180	900	269	2600	334	50000	381
60	52	180	122	360	186	950	273	2800	337	60000	381
65	55	190	127	380	191	1000	277	3000	340	70000	382
70	59	200	131	400	196	1100	284	2600	346	120000	382
75	62	210	136	420	200	1200	291	4000	350	160000	383
80	66	220	140	440	205	1300	296	4500	354	1000000	383
85	69			460	209			5000	356		

Degree of Accuracy = ±.05   Proportion of Sample Size = 0.5   Confidence Level = 95%

Another sample size table better suited for a population of 1 million or more is shown in Table 3-4.

Table 3-4. Sample Size Table for Populations of 1 Million and More

Margin of error (percent)	Confidence Level		
	99%	95%	90%
+/- 1	16,576	9,604	6,765
+/- 2	4,144	2,401	1,691
+/- 3	1,848	1,067	752
+/- 5	666	384	271

Source: Imas, L.G. and Rist, R.C. (2009). *The Road to Results.* Washington, D.C.: The World Bank.

For more complex surveys that include a variety of measures, we suggest that you refer to the books in the Additional Resources in the back of this book.

 ### Getting It Done

Now it is time to start planning your survey project. To begin, develop a one-page summary that describes the purpose of your survey: 1) list your survey objectives; 2) describe the basis for the survey (for example, literature review, focus groups, case studies, executive interest); 3) identify the target audience (if it is a complex survey and you are sampling, identify the population and sample size); and 4) describe the survey type (for example, design, instrument, and so on). Table 3-5 provides a template for your use. Table 3-6 provides a sample completed plan. You can use this plan to review the project with your stakeholders. With your plan ready, now it is time to start developing your survey.

Table 3.5. Survey Plan Template

Survey Plan	
	<Topic>
Statement of Need	
Purpose of Survey	
Broad Objectives	
Basis	
Target Audience	
Survey Type	

Table 3.6. Sample Survey Plan

Sample: Survey Plan
Evaluation of Coaching Initiative

Statement of Need	The learning and development department launched a major leadership development initiative that focuses on coaching and mentoring high-performing mid-level managers. The cost is approximately $100,000 per person to receive coaching for six months. Approximately 15 people will participate.
Purpose of Survey	The purpose of the survey is to describe the value of investing in a coaching initiative for high-performing mid-level managers.
Broad Objectives	1. Determine participant reaction to the coaching in terms of perceived value, relevance to the job, importance to job success, and recommend to other mid-level managers immediately upon completion of the coaching intervention.
	2. Determine new insights as to participant capacity to lead the organization, lead oneself, and lead others.
	3. Compare manager proficiency with eight behaviors associated with leading the organization before and after participating in the coaching initiative.
	4. Compare manager proficiency with seven behaviors associated with lead self before and after participating in the coaching initiative.
	5. Compare manager proficiency with five behaviors associated with leading others before and after the coaching initiative.
	6. Determine improvement in business measures occurring within six months after completing the coaching initiative as perceived by participants.
	7. Determine the monetary benefits of the coaching initiative and compare to investment in coaching (ROI).
Basis	Literature Review
	Primary source for leadership competencies: McCauley, C. (2006). *Developmental Assignments: Creating Learning Experiences Without Changing Jobs*. Greensboro, NC: Center for Creative Leadership Press.
	Primary source for evaluation approach: Phillips, P.P., Phillips, J.J., and Edwards, L.A. (2012). *Measuring the Success of Coaching*. Alexandria, VA: ASTD Press.
Target Audience	25 high-performing mid-level managers participating in coaching initiative.
	Immediate manager of managers participating in coaching initiative.
	Executives funding the coaching initiative.
Survey Type	Descriptive cohort study collecting data using 360-feedback questionnaire plus self-administered questionnaires pre-,during-, and post-coaching.
	Interview with managers of participants.
	Develop strategy for ensuring high response rate.

Survey Questions

■ ■

What's Inside This Chapter

In this chapter, you will learn the characteristics of good survey questions. After reading this chapter you should be able to

▶ Distinguish between the stem and the scale
▶ Address issues that affect a quality survey question
▶ Write survey questions that ask the right question the right way
▶ Develop a meaningful survey scale

Criteria for Good Survey Questions

Writing good survey questions is at the heart of survey design. To create the best survey questions, you need clear objectives that reflect specific measures. You also need a solid research design approach. But we often fail to remember that writing the actual survey questions takes time. Yes, good objectives will lead the way, and if they are SMART objectives, the survey questions literally write themselves. But still, to ensure we ask the right questions the right way, we need to take a step back and ask ourselves: Can the respondents really respond to these questions and provide us with the most reliable data possible?

There are two parts to a survey question: the stem and the scale. The stem represents the variables of interest; the scale represents the attributes we give those variables. Together they are the measures of survey objectives.

Writing good survey questions is a balance between art and science. This balance includes understanding various survey research designs and being familiar with the levels of measurement and what you can do mathematically to make meaning out of each response type. It also includes developing questions so that:

- responses reflect the data you want
- respondents understand the meaning of the question
- respondents know the answer
- respondents can answer in terms required
- respondents are willing to provide the answer.

Responses Reflect the Data You Want

A good question gets to the crux of the issue being addressed by the survey. By designing the question so that you get the answer you intend to get, you can keep the survey focused and get the information you need to serve the purpose of the survey. For example, if you are interested in knowing how much time people spend in meetings, you can ask the question multiple ways. Here are three options.

Option 1: How many meetings do you attend each month?

Option 2: On average, how many hours do you spend in meetings each week?

Option 3: On average, how long does a typical meeting last?

Option 1 may be the best measure if you want to know the frequency with which meetings occur. However, if you want to know the average number of hours spent in meetings, option 2 is the better choice. Option 3 is the better choice if you are interested in reducing the length of time the average meeting takes. Sometimes you may need to ask the questions all three ways. So the first step is to be clear about the information you need in order to take the measure you want.

Also, in writing the questions, focus on a single issue or topic within that question. For example, the question below includes two issues:

Did you think the class was informative and enjoyable?

Clearly the question is attempting to measure participants' reaction to the class; however, two measures of reaction exist in this single question: 1) participants perception of how informative the class was, and 2) participants' perception of how enjoyable the class was. This lack of focus is known as barreling. If both issues are important, then develop two question items:

▶ Do you think the class was informative?

▶ Do you think the class was enjoyable?

This common challenge in question design is often the output of weak survey objectives, hurried question development, and the desire to limit the number of questions on a survey instrument. By being clear on the information you want to gather and asking focused questions to gather that information, you will improve the reliability of the data.

Think About This

Do you want people to give you a response; or do you want them to give you the response you want?

Consider the following:

Patti spent three nights at the Crowne Plaza in Dallas, Texas. She had a successful visit with participants of the American Productivity and Quality Center (APCQ) CATALYST Project, a leadership program for K-12 school principals. Upon checkout, a nice man with a beaming smile clad in a dark suit greeted her:

Hello Dr. Phillips, did you enjoy your stay with us?

She replied: *Well, yes, I did.*

His response with rapid-fire precision: *Thank you Dr. Phillips, I'm glad you enjoyed your stay. You know, here at the Crowne Plaza we like our customers to rate us a 10 out of 10 on customer satisfaction. Would you score us a 10 today?* (big smile)

How could you say no?

Consider this: Questions designed to lead the respondent toward an answer (and getting that answer) can help you promote your cause, but do they help you know what respondents really think?

Basic Rule

Write your questions so you get the answers you seek, not the results you want.

Respondents Understand the Meaning of the Question

In order to receive accurate responses, ask questions in such a way that potential respondents consistently understand the meaning of the question. Jargon, acronyms, and cumbersome questions confuse respondents, thereby causing them to rely on their own judgment in defining the meaning of the question. And, while people may answer your question in spite of their inability to understand it, data integrity is lacking.

Here is an example of a question for which the audience may lack understanding (McMurray, 2001):

I would speak more freely if my co-workers didn't have such long left-hand columns.

Only if you are familiar with Peter Senge's mental model practices described in his book *The Fifth Discipline* and its subsequent book *The Fifth Discipline Fieldbook*, would you know what is meant by long left-hand columns. When analyzing a difficult problem such as a frustrating conversation, the participant analyzing the conversation uses the right-hand column for listing what is actually said. They use the left-hand column for writing what they think about what is said.

Even if you know the meaning of long left-hand column, the question is not ideal. A question more easily understood by the audience may be:

I would speak more freely if my co-workers were more open about what they are thinking.

Another example of a less than understandable question, also offered by McMurray (2001) is:

What is the frequency of the overall interpersonal, informal, and formal communication between the focal group and the targeted semi-autonomous, functionally specialized groups?

Can you answer this? Long, complex questions do not provide any better information than a simple, straight-to-the point question. McMurray demonstrates a clearer, more concise question as:

What is the frequency of formal communication between the focal group and your group?

Brief, clear questions give the audience opportunity to provide meaningful data. Remember, you are writing survey questions for your audience, not for you. So write them in such a way that your audience knows what you are asking.

Basic Rule
Design questions for the audience, not for you.

Respondents Know the Answer

When writing survey questions, ensure they are questions for which the audience knows the answers. There are two fundamental reasons why people may not know the answer to a question (Fowler 1995; 2009):

1. The respondent never had the information needed to answer the question.
2. The respondent had the information at some point, but is unable to recall the information accurately or in the detail required by the question.

Never Having the Information

One reason respondents may not know the answer to a survey question is that they never had the information. This is more the result of poor audience selection than question design. Sometimes researchers ask respondents to provide information about other people, such as their supervisors, colleagues, or direct reports. For example, you may administer a survey to employees asking the question:

Does your supervisor meet with each employee at the beginning of every quarter?

Unless the meeting schedule is publically announced and all employees see their colleagues come and go from the boss's office, an individual would be hard-pressed to answer that question with any level of accuracy. A better question is:

Does your supervisor meet with you at the beginning of every quarter?

Sometimes an individual has been involved in an experience, but does not have full access to the details in the form the researcher needs. For example, you might be attempting to calculate the return on investment (ROI) for a health and wellness program. You need to know how much the company saved in actual dollars due to a reduction in doctor visits as a result of the program. While participants of the program will know their level of involvement in the program and how much less time they spend at the doctor's office, they may not know how much each visit to the doctor's office actually costs the company. This is a good example of targeting the wrong source for a critical piece of information.

In both scenarios, the survey respondent doesn't know the answer, because he does not have the information.

Unable to Recall the Information

Given all of the activity we face every day, remembering specific information and behaviors is often a challenge. When designing survey questions, remember that people often don't remember, or what they do remember is more or less colorful than the actual occurrence. One solution to this problem is to administer the survey at an appropriate time given the significance of the event for which you are surveying.

For example, if you want respondents to describe what they thought about the facilitation skills of an instructor of a two-day workshop, the best time to ask is immediately. While a two-day workshop at the time seems important, in reality, the accuracy of participants' memory of that facilitator quickly fades as participants get on with their day-to-day responsibilities.

If we are trying to recall specific behaviors given a certain event, it is often challenging if the timing of that event is not readily available in our memory. For example, if a question is asked such as:

Since completing the one-day Getting Things Done® workshop, how many Fridays did you get your inbox to empty?

Think About This

Below are suggestions that will help enhance recall and time.

- Incorporate a record-keeping process into a program or project for which you know you will be surveying participants.

- Add introductory information to the survey that prepares the participants for the question.

- Ask multiple questions about the event or behavior so respondents have multiple opportunities to access their memories.

- Anchor questions in time. For example, start a question with, "In the past three months..."

- Provide lists to help jog respondents' memories.

- Place questions in a logical order or flow of events.

- Anchor questions with significant events such as holidays.

- Build a calendar or timeline into the survey.

If the workshop was conducted three months prior to administering the survey, some respondents may not be able to recall when they took the GTD® workshop. Also, while the GTD® workshop was probably a valuable investment, the respondents' ability to recall the exact frequency their inbox emptied on Fridays is limited unless supported by a calendar, timeline, or journal.

When asking questions associated with significant events, memories tend to be more reliable. For example, if you ask respondents about their activities when they purchased their first home, they are likely to remember a year or so after the event. Or if you ask respondents located in Alabama, Mississippi, or Louisiana where they were when Hurricane Katrina hit the Gulf Coast of the United States they are likely to remember, even seven years after the event. And of course, most Baby Boomers can tell you exactly where they were when John F. Kennedy was assassinated. These significant events are embedded in our memories and we can recall our behaviors, actions, and whereabouts much more easily than less significant events such as a two-day workshop. When asking questions, ask questions relevant to an event respondents actually remember and in a way that will help them remember.

Respondents Are Able to Answer in Terms Required

Write survey questions so that respondents are able to answer them in the terms required by the question. For example, when asking respondents to evaluate their ability to apply a skill or demonstrate a behavior, there is often an assumption that the situation in which they are applying that skill is stable. For example, consider the question below:

In the past 30 days, were you able to access the information you need from the knowledge management portal?

This question assumes that in the past 30 days there was no variance in the respondent's ability to access information from the knowledge management portal. Given the potential for technology failure and the variety of types of information available in a knowledge management system, this assumption may make it difficult to get a reliable response. A better approach may be to ask multiple questions about the knowledge management system to gauge the challenges people face accessing information. For example, the Likert scale is a commonly used scale to measure attitudes toward entities such as the knowledge management portal described above (as shown in Table 4-1). While a matrix of questions may lengthen the survey, it is sometimes necessary to gather the most accurate response possible.

Respondents Are Willing to Answer

Write questions so that respondents are willing to provide you the answer. Sometimes all it takes is an explanation as to why a question exists in a survey: Questions about a person's job position, salary, or eating and drinking habits are often necessary to make decisions about programs and initiatives. But potential respondents may view these questions as intrusive. By introducing the questions with an explanation as to why the data are necessary, you can ease concerns.

Table 4-1. Example of Likert Scale

Thirty days ago, we upgraded the knowledge management portal. Please rate your level of agreement with the following questions regarding your ability to access information.

	Strongly Disagree	Disagree	Neutral	Agree	Strongly Agree
Accessing information I needed using the knowledge management portal was difficult.	☐	☐	☐	☐	☐
The information I needed was easy to find using the knowledge management portal.	☐	☐	☐	☐	☐
Every time I accessed the knowledge management portal, I found the information I needed.	☐	☐	☐	☐	☐
The knowledge management portal was always available when I attempted to access information.	☐	☐	☐	☐	☐

Sometimes the question just needs a good rewrite. McMurray (2001) demonstrates this with the following question:

I frequently belittle and talk down to my fellow employees.

While a respondent might be willing to answer the question if they do belittle and talk down to their fellow employees, the likelihood of them admitting to it is slim. A better question might be:

Members of my work group show respect by eliciting each other's opinions.

Table 4-2 lists attributes of good and bad questions. Watch out for these as you write survey questions.

Table 4-2. Attributes of Good and Bad Questions

Attributes	Description	Example
Barreling vs. Specificity	Barreled questions ask respondents to rate two or more behaviors or issues in a single question. Barreling is possibly the most common problem with most survey questions. Solution: Avoid barreled questions by splitting them into multiple questions.	Bad: When making assignments, my supervisor gives clear, achievable goals that are within my control. Good: When making assignments, my supervisor gives me achievable goals.
Loose Bundling vs. Anchoring	Loose bundling occurs when questions are too general and not grounded in specific behaviors. Specific behaviors must be identified in the question. Solution: Anchor concepts in specific behaviors that can be measured or observed.	Bad: I am interested in my students. Good: I regularly share information about my students' progress with their parents.
Jargon vs. Clarity	Specialized terminology is generally not understood. Its use prevents people from understanding and answering the question responsibly. Solution: Use words frequently used in common speech. Do not assume acronyms are understood by everyone!	Bad: I would speak more freely if my co-workers didn't have such long left-hand columns. Good: I would speak more freely if my co-workers were more open about what they are thinking.
Loaded/Leading Questions vs. Fact	Loaded questions are worded to influence respondents' answers. Leading questions bias respondents' opinions. Solution: Avoid using emotionally charged wording.	Bad: The sales of automatic weapons should be banned in order to save human lives. Effective: The sales of automatic weapons should be banned.
Lack of Knowledge vs. Knowledge	Refers to when respondents either lack the knowledge necessary to accurately answer the question or have never bothered to cognitively organize their knowledge. Solution: Never ask people more than they know.	Bad: The instructor is an expert in this field. Good: The instructor effectively answered all of my questions on this topic.
Complexity vs. Simplicity	Complexity occurs when sentence phrasing is so long and labored that respondents become confused. Solution: Keep questions short and focused on single issues.	Bad: What is the frequency of the overall interpersonal, informal, and formal communication between the focal group and the targeted semi-autonomous, functionally specialized groups? Good: What is the frequency of formal communication between the focal group and your group?
Social Desirability vs. Realism	This occurs when questions have an obviously "correct" or socially desirable answer. When respondents worry about giving the "right answer" the data will be distorted. Solution: Make sure the question prompts respondents to answer with a reasoned opinion instead of an emotional response.	Bad: I frequently belittle and talk down to my fellow employees. Good: Members of my work group show respect by eliciting each other's opinions.

Source: McMurray, David P. (2001). TRAINING/Presentations. Scantron Corporation. Used with permission.

Question Response Choices

Question response choices come in a variety of formats. They can be opened or closed; they can represent qualitative measures or quantitative measures. The appropriate scale depends on the purpose of its use.

Binary/Dichotomous Scales

Dichotomous or binary scales are frequently found on surveys. These are scales where choices come down to two options. An example of a dichotomous scale is shown in Table 4-3. Dichotomous scales are closed and represent categorical or nominal data. So the results can be counted in terms of frequency with which respondents select each choice. Care must be taken when using dichotomous scales. Not all questions result in an either-or response.

Table 4-3. Binary/Dichotomous Scale
Did you register for the health and wellness workshop that is being offered on October 1?
☐ Yes   ☐ No

Multiple-Choice Scales

Multiple-choice scales, like dichotomous scales, are closed. The difference is the respondent has more than one option from which to choose. Multiple-choice scales are frequently used when capturing demographic data. These data, like the dichotomous scales, are categorical and qualitative in nature. Table 4-4 presents an example of a multiple-choice scale.

Table 4-4. Multiple-Choice Scale	
Select the type of public sector organization in which you work.	
☐ Federal	☐ Special District
☐ State	☐ City/Local
☐ County	☐ Other_____
☐ Municipal	

Think About This

Is It "Yes" or "No"?

Patti took her Land Rover in for service. She arrived early to beat the crowd. Unfortunately, the crowd had the same idea. So, upon arrival, she had to wait to speak to a service representative. By the time the rep got to her, the dealership had run out of on-site rental cars. So, the dealership bused Patti and a few other customers 20 minutes to the rental car service site. This was not a good start of the day. However, service was completed in record time. By noon, the dealership called and the vehicle was ready for pick-up. The service department took care of routine maintenance, detailed the Land Rover, and took care of a few unplanned issues. While she was not delighted with the service at first, the end result was pretty good.

The following day, Patti gets a call:

Marie: *Good morning, Dr. Phillips. This is Marie with J.D. Power. We see you recently took your Land Rover in for service.*

Patti: *Good morning, Marie. Well, yes I did.*

Marie: *That's great. Were you satisfied with your service? Yes or no?*

Patti (remembering her experience): *Well, Marie, I was not dissatisfied but I was not satisfied either.*

Marie: *I understand. Could you please answer the question as either yes or no?*

Patti: *Well, Marie, I can't. Because I was neither dissatisfied nor was I satisfied.*

Marie: *Thank you Dr. Phillips. I just need you to answer the question yes or no.*

Patti: *Well, Marie, your question is not really a yes-or-no question.*

Marie said thank you and hung up.

Almost certainly, Marie was following her script—and doing a good job. And J.D. Power clearly knows what they are doing, or they would not be the voice of the customer for so many industries and for so many decades. Had Patti answered the question "yes" or "no," it is likely Marie would have clicked the response on her computer to follow up with her standard set of questions. But in this particular situation, yes or no was not a good response choice.

Question to Think About

How could Marie have asked the question so that Patti would have an opportunity to provide an accurate measure of her level of satisfaction?

Rank Order Scales

Rank order scales allow respondents to rank in order their preferred response based on a given list of responses. An example of a rank order scale is shown in Table 4-5. Rank order scales can offer respondents the opportunity to select the one best choice or to rank all items in order of preference. They are usually closed questions and they are categorical in nature.

Table 4-5. Rank Order Scale

What is the top (number 1) barrier to changing your behavior? (Pick only the top barrier.)

☐ Time

☐ Desire

☐ Skills

☐ Other (please define)

Descriptive Scales

The most widely used scale in survey research is the descriptive scale—a scale that uses a continuum of descriptors as the response choices for a given item. These scales are used to summarize the frequency with which respondents select a particular response. But they can also be used to summarize a matrix of responses measuring similar question items, such as with the use of summated rating scales.

Descriptive scales are categorical in nature and are treated as rank order type measures, meaning that the difference in a rating has no true numerical value. However, as you will read below, this premise remains under debate. Descriptors vary depending on the objectives, but typical descriptors include agreement, frequency, satisfaction, and importance—just to name a few.

Agreement

If you have ever been involved in a survey, you are familiar with the use of agreement as a descriptor on a survey scale. Respondents are asked to indicate their agreement with a specific statement. Responses are then summarized for each question item. The most popular agreement scale is the Likert scale. In 1932, Renis Likert invented this scale to measure respondent attitudes about a specific object or observation. The typical Likert scale appears as a collection of statements about that observation reflecting favorable or unfavorable attitudes toward it. Each statement is accompanied by a graded-response rating scale using the agreement descriptor. Each response choice is anchored by a consecutive set of positive numbers indicating a progression along a continuum. While the term *Likert scale* is widely used, the genuine Likert scale meets a specific set of criteria. According to Uebersax (2006), these criteria are as follows.

1. The scale contains several items.
2. Response choices are arranged horizontally.
3. Response choices are anchored with consecutive integers.
4. Response choices are also anchored with verbal labels.
5. Verbal labels are bivalent and symmetrical about a neutral middle (meaning there is an odd number of response choices).
6. The scale measures attitude in terms of agreement/disagreement to a target statement.

A sample Likert scale is shown in Table 4-6.

Table 4-6. Sample Likert Scale

Please indicate how much you agree or disagree with the following statements:

	Strongly Disagree	Disagree	Neutral or Undecided	Agree	Strongly Agree
Executives encourage employees to exercise.	1	2	3	4	5
Managers encourage employees to exercise.	1	2	3	4	5
Co-workers encourage each other to exercise.	1	2	3	4	5

What makes the genuine Likert scale different from a typical descriptive scale question item is that the scale is the complete set of questions, and responses are summarized across all questions. The Likert item is the individual question. But the premise of the Likert scale and other similar summative rating scales is that the ultimate indicator of a respondent's attitude is found in the summation or average of all question items.

This summation and the treatment of the Likert items is under ongoing debate by researchers (Carifio and Perla, 2007; Glass et al., 1972; Jamieson, 2004; Lubke, et al., 2004). Being descriptive in nature, the question items fall into the same category of measurement as the rank order scale described above. This calls for a different type of analysis. However, because weight is given to the descriptors through the coding process, for example, 1=strongly disagree, 2=disagree, and so on, analysts often treat the scale as numerical, which lends itself to mathematical calculations, hence the ability to average response scores.

Debate aside, the Likert scale is the basis for many survey questions. The agreement scale is one of the most popular descriptive scales. But sometimes, we require other descriptors to measure what we need to measure. One other descriptor is frequency.

Frequency

Occasionally a survey question may call for a measurement of frequency. This can occur, for example, when measuring employee attitude about supervisor behavior or measuring an employee's application of newly acquired knowledge and skill. Frequency descriptors can indicate specific time intervals or can be held to a more general concept of time. For example, your company has implemented a health and wellness program. Through program implementation, you teach them the importance of walking every day and offer a list of challenges to participants. To keep them motivated, you provide a wellness journal so they can track food and beverage intake as well as their progress with walking. Specific challenges include:

- ▸ Walk 10,000 steps every day.
- ▸ Wear your pedometer every time you walk.
- ▸ Keep track of the number of steps you walk every day.
- ▸ Keep track of the number of calories burned by walking every day.
- ▸ List the foods you eat in your wellness journal every day.
- ▸ List the beverages you drink in your wellness journal every day.

An important measure of success is the frequency with which participants achieve these objectives. A potential scale for this line of questioning might look like the one shown in Table 4-7.

A challenge when developing frequency scales that measure specific time intervals is the assumption that the noted behavior is regular. It could be that during one week, participants did walk 10,000 steps every day; however, the next week they did not. Pegging the frequency to a specific time period with more general time intervals may be a better approach, as shown in Table 4-8.

Table 4-7. Sample Frequency Scale: Specific Time Intervals

Please rate the frequency with which you do the following:

	Never	One to Two Days a Week	Three to Four Days a Week	Five to Six Days a Week	Every Day
Walk 10,000 steps in one day.	☐	☐	☐	☐	☐
Wear your pedometer when you walk.	☐	☐	☐	☐	☐
Log the number of steps you walk in a day.	☐	☐	☐	☐	☐
Log the number of calories burned by walking each day.	☐	☐	☐	☐	☐
List in your wellness journal the foods you eat.	☐	☐	☐	☐	☐
List in your wellness journal the beverages you drink.	☐	☐	☐	☐	☐

Table 4-8. Sample Frequency Scale: General Time Intervals

Please rate the frequency with which you do the following:

	Never	Rarely	Occasionally	Fairly Often	Very Often
Walk 10,000 steps in one day.	☐	☐	☐	☐	☐
Wear your pedometer when you walk.	☐	☐	☐	☐	☐
Log the number of steps you walk in a day.	☐	☐	☐	☐	☐
Log the number of calories burned by walking each day.	☐	☐	☐	☐	☐
List in your wellness journal the foods you eat.	☐	☐	☐	☐	☐
List in your wellness journal the beverages you drink.	☐	☐	☐	☐	☐

Noted

1. People taking aptitude tests are often taught never to answer "always" or "never." However, "always" or "never" are reasonable answers that researchers may want to identify.

2. The scale that uses proportion of time, such as "more than half the time" or "less than half the time," may be less subject to individual variability in interpretation of adjectives than the other scales. Scales that are quantifiable, as compared with those that rely purely on adjectives, also have advantages in translations across languages.

3. Scales of frequency pose difficulty in defining the middle or intermediate categories. "Usually" or "always" on the positive end and "rarely" or "never" on the negative end are relatively well defined. However, terms like "some of the time" or "fairly often" are more difficult to work with in the middle of a continuum of frequency.

Source: Fowler, F.J. (1995). *Improving Survey Questions*. Thousand Oaks: Sage Publications.

Satisfaction

Measuring satisfaction is common in most organizations. In the learning and development field, satisfaction measurement often occurs at the end of a workshop. Meetings and events professionals might measure satisfaction at the end of a conference. Human resources professionals are often charged with measuring employee satisfaction with the workplace, their jobs, and the opportunities provided through the workplace. Fundamentally, "satisfaction" is a measure of the relationship between what people want and what people get.

An example of a satisfaction scale is shown in Table 4-9.

As shown in Table 4-9, the progression of satisfaction goes from very dissatisfied to very satisfied with a neutral response for those participants who are neither dissatisfied nor satisfied. In the next section, we will cover the issue of the middle option as well as the number of choices and scale direction. But for now, the point is to focus on the continuum. As with all scales, the continuum must be evident.

A key issue to remember when considering a satisfaction scale is that it should only be asked when respondents have some kind of expectation about the event, behavior, or phenomenon. If you think your respondents have no real expectation about the issue, use a more appropriate scale.

Table 4-9. Sample Satisfaction Scale

During the workshop, how satisfied were you with the following:

	Very Dissatisfied	Somewhat Dissatisfied	Neither Dissatisfied or Satisfied	Fairly Often	Very Often
Facilitator's ability to answer your questions	☐	☐	☐	☐	☐
Facilitator's ability to cover content as planned	☐	☐	☐	☐	☐
Relevance of the content to your job	☐	☐	☐	☐	☐
Quality of the workshop materials	☐	☐	☐	☐	☐

Basic Rule

Use "satisfaction" scales only when respondents have an expectation about what they are observing.

Importance

Scales of importance are useful when assessing the need for a program, project, event, or initiative. It is also useful when gauging motivating factors that drive employee or customer satisfaction. For example, the learning and development team of a large pharmaceutical company is considering changing its content delivery for a major program. A scale they might use to measure the importance of the elements in the current program is shown in Table 4-10.

Quantity

Measuring quantity in the generic sense is common in survey research. For example, in program evaluation we often ask questions about the increase in the performance of a particular business measure or the decrease in a particular non-productive behavior. When assessing organizational needs, it is often important to ask questions about the size of a gap in performance, which lends itself to a scale representative of quantity. Table 4-11 demonstrates the use of a scale measuring quantity.

Table 4-10. Sample Importance Scale

Please rate each element of the MDX program in terms of its importance to the learning process.

	Very Unimportant	Unimportant	Neither Important or Unimportant	Important	Very Important
Face-to-face interaction with other participants	☐	☐	☐	☐	☐
Face-to-face interaction with instructor	☐	☐	☐	☐	☐
Multiple-part case study	☐	☐	☐	☐	☐
Team assignments	☐	☐	☐	☐	☐
Access to online resources	☐	☐	☐	☐	☐

Table 4-11. Sample Quantity Scale

Consider the following characteristics regarding the governance of the organization. Indicate how much each characteristic has increased or decreased since 2009.

	Decreased a Lot	Decreased Some	About the Same	Increased Some	Increased a Lot
Transparent	☐	☐	☐	☐	☐
Fair	☐	☐	☐	☐	☐
Equitable to all members	☐	☐	☐	☐	☐
Representative	☐	☐	☐	☐	☐
Accountable	☐	☐	☐	☐	☐
Strategic	☐	☐	☐	☐	☐
Efficient	☐	☐	☐	☐	☐

Evaluative Scales

Another common scale is one associated with evaluative questions. These questions ask respondents to evaluate a project, event, or other phenomenon. While satisfaction scales are evaluative in a sense, they are comparing satisfaction with what the respondent expected and what they received. Evaluative questions do not measure the satisfaction with an object or event, but rather the general perception someone has about that phenomenon. For example, your organization is planning to invest in SMART Board technology, specifically, the 885ix interactive whiteboard system. The plan is to place one whiteboard system into each classroom. You are in charge of the pilot test and you want to measure the effectiveness of the tool in supporting facilitators in the two classrooms in which SMART Boards are currently installed. To take the measurement, you might develop a set of evaluative questions as shown in Table 4-12.

Table 4-12. Sample Evaluative Scale

Considering the following features of the SMART Board currently installed in your classroom, how do you rate the effectiveness of these features in supporting you in facilitation of workshops?

	Poor	Fair	Satisfactory	Good	Excellent
Touch recognition	☐	☐	☐	☐	☐
Onscreen keyboard	☐	☐	☐	☐	☐
Freestyle interaction	☐	☐	☐	☐	☐
SMART Meeting Pro software	☐	☐	☐	☐	☐
HD-ready projector	☐	☐	☐	☐	☐
Action tracking technology	☐	☐	☐	☐	☐

While not all-inclusive, additional examples of descriptive scales using evaluative descriptions are shown in Table 4-13.

Table 4-13. Sample Evaluative Scale Descriptions

Less Than Acceptable	Acceptable	More Than Acceptable
☐	☐	☐

Does Not Meet Standards	Meets Standards	Exceed Standards
☐	☐	☐

Very Effective	Effective	Ineffective	Very Ineffective
☐	☐	☐	☐

Poor	Fair	Good	Very Good	Excellent
☐	☐	☐	☐	☐

Poor	Fair	Satisfactory	Good	Excellent
☐	☐	☐	☐	☐

As mentioned earlier, the descriptive scale is the most commonly used scale in survey research. Response choices run the gamut. The examples presented here provide just a few of the descriptors available to support the use of this type of scale. In the Additional Resources section of this book you will find the URL for a summary of different types of scale response choices. Dr. Del Siegle in the Department of Education at the University of Connecticut developed this list.

Numerical Scales

Numerical scales are those scales in which response choices are numerical, albeit there may or may not be a true zero. Numerical scales may be anchored by descriptors at either end of the scale to provide a basis for the highest (positive) or lowest (negative) response. Table 4-14 provides a typical numerical scale using "unimportant" and "important" as the anchors. The scale represents a continuum of response choices moving from lowest to highest score. This scale provides a numerical gradient on which respondents can make their choice. Its usefulness beyond the descriptive scale is that a numerical difference between responses can be reported. However, it is a scale for which there is no true zero, meaning, from a mathematical perspective, results are limited to frequencies, addition, and subtraction. For example, while 1 is the lowest rating of importance (unimportant), and the difference between response choices 1 and 2 is clearly 1 (2 – 1 = 1), a person who rates "importance" a 2, is not saying that she believes the activity is twice as important as one who rates the activity a 1. The rating of 2 merely indicates that the respondent rates the activity of greater importance by 1 point.

Table 4-14. Sample Numerical Scale: True Zero Does Not Exist

Using the scale below, please tell us how important measures of organizational outcomes are to the following (1 = Unimportant; 5 = Important).

	1	2	3	4	5
Improving processes to track participant progression with skills	☐	☐	☐	☐	☐
Building stronger commitment to the program by key stakeholders	☐	☐	☐	☐	☐

A numerical scale for which there is a true zero is one where the numbers have real mathematical meaning (you can add, subtract, multiply, and divide). For example, if your objective is to determine the average number of days respondents participate in the specific challenge areas identified in the health and wellness workshop, you would use a 0- to 7-point scale. This numerical scale has meaning beyond a typical 1 to 5 scale in that there is a meaningful zero. Zero in this case means that respondents did not complete the challenge on any number of days. Scores 1-7 represent the number of days in a week. Table 4-15 presents this numerical scale.

Unlike the scale in Table 4-14, when a person scores a 2 on this scale, the score is actually two times more than a score of 1. If the respondents keep up their wellness log and refer to it when answering this question, this average should be reliable.

Numerical scales are useful, but because the numbers themselves are sometimes arbitrary (no true zero) it is helpful to use descriptors to provide meaning to the choices along the scale. Combining numbers and descriptors is especially helpful when measuring perceptions of behavior. The number provides the rating of behavior, but the descriptors give meaning to those numbers. An example of such a scale is the behaviorally anchored numerical scale.

Table 4-15. Sample Numerical Scale: True Zero Exists

On average, how many days per week did you do the following since completing the workshop?

	Days Per Week							
	0	1	2	3	4	5	6	7
Walk 10,000 steps in one day.	☐	☐	☐	☐	☐	☐	☐	☐
Wear your pedometer when you walk.	☐	☐	☐	☐	☐	☐	☐	☐
Log the number of steps you walk in a day.	☐	☐	☐	☐	☐	☐	☐	☐
Log the number of calories burned by walking each day.	☐	☐	☐	☐	☐	☐	☐	☐
List in your wellness journal the foods you eat.	☐	☐	☐	☐	☐	☐	☐	☐
List in your wellness journal the beverages you drink.	☐	☐	☐	☐	☐	☐	☐	☐

Behaviorally Anchored Numerical Scale

Behaviorally anchored numerical scales are effective scales in measuring the behavioral performance of others as well as that of oneself. These scales use a numeric rating system, but the numerical choices are anchored by specific behaviors that progress toward the ideal behavior (Shrock and Coscarelli, 2007).

For example, behaviorally anchored numerical scales may be helpful in measuring a retail salesperson's performance when a customer asks for assistance. Using a scale of 1 to 5, the sales representatives are rated on their performance. Each response choice is anchored by a description of the performance with that behavior. For example a rating of 1 is the least preferred level of performance and may be an appropriate rating when the sales representative uses a curt voice or even ignores the request. The best performance, a rating of 5, is when a sales representative responds immediately to the request with a warm and welcoming voice. Ratings of 2, 3, and 4 are also anchored in specific descriptions of the performance related to the particular behavior under assessment. Table 4-16 provides an example of a behaviorally anchored numerical scale.

Table 4-16. Sample Behaviorally Anchored Numerical Scale

Behavior	Performance	Rating
Response to request for assistance	Uses curt voice tone or ignores request	1
	Delays request using a neutral voice tone	2
	Responds when approached by customer using a neutral voice tone	3
	Approaches the customer offering assistance, using a neutral voice tone	4
	Approaches the customer offering assistance, using a warm, welcoming voice tone	5

Developing behaviorally anchored numerical scales is challenging and takes time. The key is to ensure that if two or more people are rating a person's performance using the scale, the scale is written so clearly that both observers rate the performance the same. This helps ensure reliability of ratings of performance by other people and also when people are rating their own performance using the same type of scale.

Open-Ended Scales

Open-ended scales allow researchers to explore issues whereas closed questions, such as those described above, provide important data that are analyzed through statistics. Open-ended scales provide a qualitative look at an issue; however, open-ended questions can also allow respondents to provide numerical data. Table 4-17 provides an example of open-ended questions that provide both qualitative and quantitative data.

Other Interesting Scales

Many other types of scales than those previously mentioned are available. Some of these scales may be useful to you. For example, the semantic differential scale measures attitudes using polar adjectives such as "adequate–inadequate," "good–evil," or "important–unimportant." It measures meanings of things and concepts and is routinely used in measuring attitude. Respondents are first given a concept. Then, using a set of polar adjectives, they rate their attitude toward one of the extremes. Semantic differential scales are useful in marketing, personality measurement, operations research, communications, clinical psychology, and other areas. While they are similar to Likert, the difference is that the classic Likert scale measures attitude using a rank-order type response choice, even though response choices are sometimes combined with a number to support the evidence of the continuum. The semantic differential scales measure the difference in attitude using a numerical scale anchored in adjectives that describe polar opposite attitudes toward a concept or object.

Table 4-17. Sample Open-Ended Questions to Capture Qualitative and Quantitative Data

Important Questions to Ask on Feedback Questionnaires

Planned Improvements

Please indicate how you will use the content from this program.

1. _____

2. _____

3. _____

As a result of this application, please estimate the impact (i.e., increased sales, reduced absenteeism, reduced employee complaints, improved quality, increased personal effectiveness, etc.) over a period of one year._____

Estimate the monetary benefits for this impact. _____

What is the basis of this estimate? _____

What confidence, expressed as a percentage, can you put in your estimate? (0%=No Confidence; 100%=Certainty) _____%

Source: Phillips, P.P. and Phillips, J.J. (2007). *The Value of Learning: How Organizations Capture Value and ROI and Translate it into Support, Improvement, and Funds.* San Francisco: Pfeiffer.

The Stapel scale is a unipolar 10-point rating scale developed by Jan Stapel. Unlike the semantic differential scale where there are two words or phrases anchoring the scale, the Stapel scale only uses one word or phrase. If the survey respondent has a negative preference toward the item, then they mark a negative rating; if they have a positive preference, they mark a positive rating. Stapel scales are often used in marketing research when investigating customers' attitudes toward products and services. However, they are also used in measuring attitude and preferences toward experiences, learning, engaging with others, and more.

The visual analog scale is a response scale that measures attitudes and perceptions along a continuous scale. This format presents respondents with a continuous line between a pair of descriptors representing opposite ends of a continuum. The respondent places a mark at a point on the line that represents her opinion, attitude, belief, or whatever is being measured. Pain surveys are a classic example of the use of visual analog scales. An advantage of the visual analog scale is that the scoring is based on a continuous scale, meaning that the scale itself is sensitive to the response; whereas, the typical Likert-type scale relies on discrete inputs from the respondents. A disadvantage is that different analysts may interpret marks on the line differently. Technology helps us with this by using mathematical algorithms to value marks along the line. Table 4-18 presents examples of each of these scales.

Table 4-18. Additional Scales

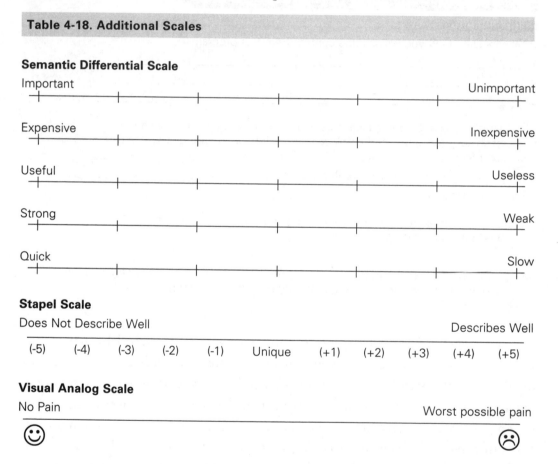

There are still many other scaling methods based on both item-response theory and classic measurement theory. Which scale you use depends on the purpose of the survey and the specific objectives you are trying to achieve. In the Additional Resources section in the back of the book, you will find resources to help you learn more about scale development and the theories that support them.

Think About This

Many people ask whether or not N/A (not applicable) is a good response choice. As with all questions regarding survey design, the answer is, it depends. On one hand, if you are surveying a group of people who have experienced the program or event for which you are surveying, then N/A is inappropriate because you should only ask relevant questions. On the other hand, if you are surveying a large group about several issues and some people in the group have not had the opportunity to engage in the issue, N/A may be an appropriate response. But don't add N/A just to give people an out.

As for the "Don't Know" response, if potential respondents "don't know" the answer to a survey question, they are likely not the right audience for the question.

Challenges With Developing Scales

Scale development is not as easy as just deciding to use Likert, numerical, or open-ended. Thought must go into it, and in the ideal case, a bit of analysis to ensure the scale reliably measures what it is intended to measure. A few basic considerations when developing scales are variance, discrimination, accuracy, symmetry, and direction.

Variance

Variance refers to the number of response choices in a scale. Variability is a good quality in scales. The more variance in the response scale, the more opportunities you have to correlate the survey item with other survey items. One way to ensure greater variability is to increase the number of response choices. However, if you have a relatively long questionnaire with a numerical scale of 0 to 100, for example, response fatigue is likely to set in. Using a scale such as the visual analog scale can provide an optimum number of response options because respondents can mark anywhere on the line and the value of the mark is determined using a real number. But, when considering using scales with an infinite number of response choices, you must ask yourself (and your team) two questions: 1) How precise do the responses need to be, given the purpose of the survey? 2) Do we have the resources (capability, time, money) to analyze the data appropriately?

A set of discrete response choices (such as Likert-type descriptive scale) can often provide "good enough" reliability to make sound judgment about the measures; and in many cases they are the best scale given the survey objectives. But, even with discrete scales, there is often debate over the appropriate number of response choices. In addition, argument over whether odd- or even-numbered scales are better is routine in many organizations. If the scale is anchored in polar opposite descriptors, such as "strongly dissatisfied" and "strongly satisfied," the middle score gives the individual who is neither satisfied nor dissatisfied an opportunity to provide an accurate measure of their position. If everyone in your sample opts for the middle ground, they are sending you as strong a message as if they selected one extreme or the other. On the other hand, even numbered scales do force the respondent to make a commitment one way or the other—even if it is a weak commitment.

Discrimination

Discrimination refers to the respondent's ability to distinguish between each response choice. While variability in response choices is a good quality, if the respondent can more easily distinguish between 4 and 5 versus 99 and 100, are you doing the scale (and the respondent) justice by using a 0- to 100-point scale? Also, when offering too many descriptive response choices, it is likely respondents will be unable to distinguish between them. Finally, poor word choice for descriptors can interfere with respondents' ability to discriminate between response choices. For example, can you discriminate between the response choices in the following scale?

Practically None	A Few	About Half	Many	Practically All
☐	☐	☐	☐	☐

Some people would say no. What is the difference between "Practically None" and "A Few?" Could "About Half" be closer to "A Few" than it is to "Many" and vice versa? Respondents should be able to see the progress toward agreement or disagreement, positive or negative, and so on. Consider the following two scales, Scale A and Scale B. How easy is it for you to discriminate between response choices for each?

Scale A

Some	Few	Many	None	Very Few
☐	☐	☐	☐	☐

Scale B

Many	Some	Few	Very Few	None
☐	☐	☐	☐	☐

Most people would say Scale B provides a better opportunity to respond accurately.

Issues with variance and discrimination are important considerations when developing scales. But, if the scale is inaccurate, what value does addressing them add?

Accuracy

Along with variance and discrimination, accuracy is a critical factor to consider when developing scales. The key question here is: Does your scale accurately reflect the measure you are purporting to take? If you are asking someone to report on frequency, your scale should reflect measures of frequency. If you are asking evaluative questions, such as the quality of facilitation, use scales that accurately evaluate facilitation. If you are asking questions of agreement, use an agreement scale. For example, do you see an opportunity to improve the following descriptors, given the question stem?

	Disagree				Agree
	1	2	3	4	5
How effectively did you apply the knowledge/skills learned during the program?	☐	☐	☐	☐	☐

The question asks respondents to rate effectiveness; however, the scale descriptors are agreement. Accurate assignment of attributes given the variable in question is important. Ensure you get the scale right.

Symmetry

Symmetry is another word for balance. Each option should be proportional to the others. A four-point scale should reflect four even parts. Of the four scales provided by McMurray (2001) below, which do you think is most balanced?

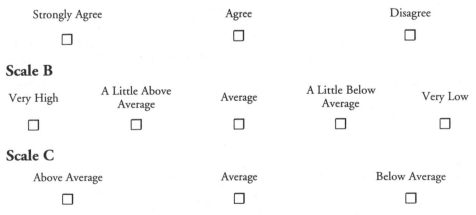

Scale A

Strongly Agree	Agree	Disagree
☐	☐	☐

Scale B

Very High	A Little Above Average	Average	A Little Below Average	Very Low
☐	☐	☐	☐	☐

Scale C

Above Average	Average	Below Average
☐	☐	☐

Scale D

Excellent	Very Good	Good	Fair	Poor
☐	☐	☐	☐	☐

Of the four scales shown, Scale A is out of balance as it is missing a response choice "Strongly Disagree." Scale B and Scale C are most balanced in that there are polar opposite response choices to the extremes. However, overall, Scale B is probably not a good set of response choices because of the vagueness around "A Little Above" and "A Little Below" and the inability to differentiate between the response choices. Scale D is a good scale given that the continuum from good to poor is evident.

Direction

Direction is an issue that comes up routinely when developing scales for survey questions. Should we go high-to-low or low-to-high? Many researchers suggest that direction biases survey response. If the more positive response choice is closest to the stem, the theory is that people will more likely check the more positive box. According to Fink (2003), scale direction is most important in face-to-face interviews and least important in anonymous, self-administered questionnaires. If the scale is measuring something important to the respondent, direction probably doesn't matter at all.

One example of the importance of scale direction on a self-administered questionnaire is when the question leads to a response that can be potentially embarrassing for the respondent. If the least negative response is placed first, the respondent may select that response because it is the least embarrassing. For example, Table 4-19 presents a matrix with three questions that could, if the respondent were honest, embarrass him if anyone tied that response to his name.

Table 4-19. Potentially Embarrassing Survey Questions

	Very Much (4)	Much (3)	A Fair Amount (2)	A Little (1)	Not at All (0)
I am afraid to question my client's opinion.	☐	☐	☐	☐	☐
I frequently feel anxious before speaking in front of large groups.	☐	☐	☐	☐	☐
I am uncomfortable coaching my employees.	☐	☐	☐	☐	☐

Noted

Arlene Fink (2003) provides the following guidelines for developing scales:

- 5- to 7-point scales are adequate for the majority of surveys that use ordered responses.

- Self-administered questionnaires and telephone interviews should probably use 4- to 5-point scales.

- In-person interviews should use visual aids for scales with five or more points on them.

- For questions that are potentially embarrassing or that ask about socially undesirable behaviors or attitudes, consider putting the negative end of the scale first.

- Deciding which end of the scale to place first is most important in face-to-face interviews and least important in anonymous self-administered and other mail surveys.

Getting It Done

This chapter provided a lot of information about survey questions. There is still much more you can learn. Refer to the resources in the back of the book to get more technical detail about designing survey questions.

In the meantime, it is time to start writing your survey questions. If you developed survey objectives as you read about in chapter 2, you are well on your way.

To get started, make your list of survey questions (you will lay them out on the survey instrument in chapter 5). As you develop the questions, ask yourself the questions shown in Table 4-20.

Table 4-20. Questions to Consider as You Develop Survey Questions

1. Does the question reflect the data I want based on the survey objective?
2. Is the question clear enough that all respondents can answer it?
3. Will respondents know the answer to this question?
4. Will respondents be able to answer the question in terms I need them to answer it, given the research objectives?
5. Will respondents be willing to answer this question?
6. Does the scale reflect enough response choices, without having too many?
7. Will respondents be able to discriminate between response choices?
8. Does the scale accurately reflect what I am trying to measure?
9. Is the scale symmetrical (balanced)?
10. Is the direction of the scale appropriate for the question?
11. Given the purpose and objectives of this survey, will my survey questions allow respondents the opportunity to provide the most accurate response possible?

5

Survey Instrument Design

■ ■

What's Inside This Chapter

The format, design, and implementation of a survey play a key role in determining the survey's success with gathering quality and quantity of data. Upon completing this chapter, you will be able to:

▶ Capture reliable responses
▶ Easily tabulate survey responses
▶ Address validity and reliability issues
▶ Address ethical issues

Questionnaire Format

Chapter 4 focused on the types of survey questions. This chapter focuses on the design of the questionnaire itself, addressing issues of format, design, and implementation of the questionnaire. It begins with a look at questionnaire format. A few issues are important in ensuring that questionnaires are formatted properly and designed for easy tabulation.

Vertical vs. Horizontal

There are two basic layouts for questions on the self-administered questionnaire where response choices are pre-coded. Responses can be inserted vertically, as shown in Figure 5-1, or horizontally, as shown in Figure 5-2.

Figure 5-1. Vertical Format

Please indicate the extent of use of the counseling skills when there is an unplanned absence:

☐ With every absence

☐ About 80% of the time

☐ About 50% of the time

☐ About 20% of the time

☐ Rarely, if ever

Figure 5-2. Horizontal Format

Please indicate the frequency with which you use the skills from this program:

☐ Very Frequently   ☐ Frequently   ☐ Occasionally   ☐ Rarely   ☐ Never

While the horizontal format may be more compact and can reduce the length of the questionnaire, the vertical option is usually recommended. The horizontal option can cause confusion as respondents may improperly check or circle a response. With the vertical option, this is less likely. Also, the vertical option will yield fewer errors during tabulation since the person entering the data will be working from a list versus working across. A potential exception to this recommendation is when yes or no responses are needed. A dichotomous response scale (yes or no) is generally better positioned in horizontal format. The possibility of errors is minimized. Of course, if using electronic survey tools, layout does not affect tabulation, although it may still affect the response.

Grids

Grids or matrixes can provide an efficient way to offer responses for a series of related questions. For example, Figure 5-3 shows a grid of related questions that will help the researcher determine measures that are potentially linked to a program. Grids make the survey efficient for responses. It clusters the related topics together and usually provides for easy response. However, if the grid gets too complex, it can become a challenge for respondents. Grids that are too long often cause respondents to lose interest.

Figure 5-3. Example of a Grid

Indicate the extent to which you think this program influences each of these measures in your branch.

	No Influence	Limited Influence	Moderate Influence	Much Influence	Very Much Influence
	1	2	3	4	5
a. New accounts	☐	☐	☐	☐	☐
b. Sales	☐	☐	☐	☐	☐
c. Customer response time	☐	☐	☐	☐	☐
d. Cross-sales ratio	☐	☐	☐	☐	☐
e. Cost control	☐	☐	☐	☐	☐
f. Employee satisfaction	☐	☐	☐	☐	☐
g. Customer satisfaction	☐	☐	☐	☐	☐
h. Customer complaints	☐	☐	☐	☐	☐
i. Customer loyalty	☐	☐	☐	☐	☐

Font

The font used in a questionnaire should be clean, crisp, and professional in appearance. Unusual designs, including those that mimic handwriting, should not be used in a professional survey. When selecting a font for use in a professional survey or questionnaire, it is important to ensure that it is readable in both digital and paper formats. Avoid fonts that are hard to read, bold, or too small. The more difficult the survey is to read, the less likely it will be completed and returned. Also, take care when using special fonts within specific questions, as it can influence the response. For example, the question:

"The candidate positively influenced my decision."

elicits a different response than:

"The candidate **positively** influenced my opinion."

Noted

According to a recent survey, the best fonts to use for paper-based surveys are Times New Roman and Garamond. The best fonts for online use are Arial, Courier, and Verdana.

Source: American Writers and Artists, Incorporated, www.awaionline.com.

Spacing

There are two spacing issues around the question format. First is within the question itself, particularly when using a grid. At least one space should be allowed within various responses to reduce the likelihood of making mistakes in the response. Also, questions should have at least two to three spaces between each so the respondent can clearly see when they have moved on to another question. Like font, spacing should be considered for all mediums of delivery.

Paper

The paper selected for hard-copy questionnaires should be professional, crisp, and conducive for responses. The weight of the paper should not be so light that it wrinkles easily, but not so heavy that it becomes cumbersome to complete and return. If the questionnaire is to be delivered in hard copy, always view a sample before sending it to respondents.

Consistency

The design, spacing, and font of questions should be consistent throughout the entire survey. This creates a flow and makes the questionnaire easier to follow. Consistency is the key for giving the document a professional appearance. Ideally, the same types of questions (Likert, binomial, open-ended, and so on) should be grouped together to ensure consistency.

Bold and Underlining

The use of bold typeface can bring out key issues if it is used consistently throughout the questionnaire. Underlining can have the same effect but generally does not attract the same attention. Sometimes underlining can make the survey appear cluttered and unprofessional. The key is that both approaches can be used to bring attention, but overuse can cause the opposite effect and cause the text to become less meaningful.

As previously mentioned, highlighting specific words in a question can sometimes influence the response, so take care when using bold and underlining.

Think About This

Consistency is key in developing a professional, successful survey. If the survey has multiple authors, or is developed over a period of time, be sure to read and test it in its entirety before distributing it to respondents. This will help ensure consistent tone, flow, and appearance of the survey instrument.

Length

The length of the instrument presents a dilemma common among designers of questionnaires and surveys. Ideally, the shorter the survey, the higher response rates will be. However, if a significant amount of detail is needed, it may be necessary to have a five- to 10-page instrument for a comprehensive survey project. If at all possible, questionnaires should be kept to five pages or fewer. If they are longer than that, special techniques presented in chapter 7 will help increase response rates. The length of the instrument is not as critical as the time needed to complete it. Sometimes, a five-page survey can be completed in 15 minutes because of the use of pre-coded questions and forced-choice options.

Preparation for Analysis

An often overlooked issue is designing the survey or questionnaire for ease of tabulation. If ignored, this can make the analysis more expensive and time consuming, and can also lead to difficulties with presenting the data. Technology has helped with this issue, as survey tools typically have at least a fundamental data analysis package. At the very least, data from surveys can be downloaded in an appropriate format for whatever data analysis package you use. But, there are still occasions when paper-based surveys are most appropriate; therefore, consider formatting the survey with data analysis in mind.

>
> ## Basic Rule
> When designing any type of survey, begin with the end in mind, considering the type of data required for the survey objectives as well as ease for respondents. Even if a survey is aesthetically perfect, if the results are difficult or impossible to analyze, the survey will not serve its intended purpose.

Closed vs. Open-Ended Questions

As mentioned in chapter 4, there are a variety of response choices that can be used in a survey. Which one you use depends on the survey objectives, specific measures, and analysis that's required to provide the information stakeholders need. Closed-ended questions, such as yes/no, descriptive and numerical scales, multiple-choice responses, matching, and ranking responses all provide respondents the easiest approach to answering survey questions. They are also the easiest for analysis and reporting. So, closed-ended questions tend to be preferred over open-ended ones.

Open-ended questions such as responses requiring sentence completion, one to three sentences, one-page responses, or essays are often more difficult to analyze and tabulate correctly. They also leave room for misinterpretation of results. However, there is a place for verbatim data. For example, when asking how a person is using new leader behavior, open-ended questions can provide insight into specific issues. This type of data can be analyzed and categorized as themes can be developed and reported.

The difficulty of having closed-ended questions only is that they often leave few options for responses that go beyond the predetermined categories. Follow-up to statistical surveys with focus groups and interviews can help interpret quantitative findings. However, this increases the cost of data collection. Providing a space for comments or other items at the end of each question can be helpful.

Electronic Tabulation

When using paper-based surveys, tabulation can be accomplished using scanning equipment. Scanning equipment has continued to evolve and can be helpful when tabulating the data and developing subsequent tables and charts. Web-based surveys have streamlined tabulation. Many commercially available surveys will tabulate responses and develop appropriate charts, tables, and other graphic organizers to add professional and aesthetic interest to survey results.

Preparing for Analysis

Instrument design plays an important role in preparing for analysis. The safe way to approach this process is to examine every question with the point of view of how it would be tabulated, summarized, and reported to the audience. When several questions are clustered or linked, thinking through how they will be presented is critical. Paying appropriate attention to this can be valuable in managing total time and cost involved in the survey project and will often reduce frustration of those who must process the data. All of this effort is taken to prevent the comment, "I wish I had thought about the results and reporting at the time I designed my questions and questionnaire."

Layout and Design

The flow of the questionnaire should be carefully planned with logical and rational sequencing. At the same time, the survey must attract attention and display professionalism. Here are a few tips.

Flow and Sequencing

The flow of the questionnaire should generally follow one of three approaches to sequencing. A first option is to order the questions based on the difficulty of the response, starting with the easiest and moving to the most difficult (or moving from the most difficult to the least difficult) and keeping that order throughout. The use of this approach is dependent on the length of the questionnaire or survey and the particular audience for which the survey is designed.

A second approach is to place the sequencing in the logical order that the study results will unfold, letting the survey tell the story as respondents read the questions. Using this logical flow as the blueprint for survey design will not only be helpful in the analysis, but also in the respondents' view of the survey itself.

Figure 5-4 shows a questionnaire that is designed to capture the success of a leadership development program. The questions move through four logical levels of data, beginning with the reaction to the questionnaire and migrating through the learning that has taken place. Next, the application of the leadership skills is explored and finally the consequence or impact of the skills is determined. It helps respondents logically see how their success has unfolded in the program, as they reacted, learned, applied, and had an impact with their leadership skills.

Designing survey instruments using a logical flow is the desired approach because it helps guide the respondent through the preferred course of action and often helps remind them of the processes as they are providing data. It also ensures results are reported in the same logical way so stakeholders can get a clear picture of the findings.

Figure 5-4. Sequencing in Order of Flow of Events

Leadership and Performance Questionnaire						

Please use the following scale for each item:

1 Not at all	2	3 Somewhat	4	5 Very much

Reaction: 1

Provide your perception of the following to describe the program:

	1	2	3	4	5
A. Relevance to my work					
B. Important to my success					
C. I intend to use the content					

Learning: 2

Indicate the extent to which you learned in the program:

	1	2	3	4	5
A. Problem solving, when needed					
B. Counseling, when necessary					
C. Goal setting, at least					
D. Motivating the average performer					
E. Recognizing performance					

Application: 3

Indicate the extent to which you applied the skills learned in the program:

	1	2	3	4	5
A. Problem solving, when needed					
B. Counseling, when necessary					
C. Goal setting, at least					
D. Motivating the average performer					
E. Recognizing performance					

Impact: 4

Indicate the extent to which the use of skills from this program has improved the following measures:

	1	2	3	4	5
A. Productivity of the team					
B. Quality of work					
C. Job engagement					
D. Retention of team managers					

A third approach to sequencing is through the series of different types of data. For example, soft, qualitative data may be separated from the quantitative data, or test data may be separated from the perception data. This has the advantage of tracing through the various types of data and giving different viewpoints of the situation and the data at the end.

The key is to follow some logic in the flow and sequencing of the data. It is important to think about the beginning of the survey to clearly present data sets that will capture the attention and interest of the respondent. The ending of the survey should always leave a place open for the respondent to make comments about the project. This space allows for the respondent to do the following:

▸ Supply data not asked for in the survey, eliciting unplanned observations.

▸ Provide ways in which the target of the survey can be improved. Suggestions for improvements are excellent process improvement opportunities.

▸ Allow for additional comments about the issue under study. This is often a sound-off opportunity as respondents may offer a variety of comments that can be insightful and helpful.

Attractiveness

The survey must be attractive and appealing to respondents. It must be eye-catching, easy to read, and able to hold the interest of the respondent as much as possible. Illustrations can be helpful if they draw interest and help hold attention. The entire process must be professional. It should have a serious slant about it, because after all, if an investment is being made in the survey project, it must be a serious project, right? Sometimes, the use of color can be helpful, as the colors can draw attention to the questionnaire or to certain parts of it.

Some annual or routine surveys use a particular color, for example, and it often becomes part of the brand. One organization has an annual employee feedback survey that is distributed on pink paper and it is regarded as the "pink sheet" survey. Colors should not detract from the professionalism of the survey, but should be used in a tasteful way to attract and retain the interest of the respondents throughout the process.

Correspondence

The correspondence that precedes or accompanies the questionnaire is critical to the success of the survey project. These correspondence opportunities must be carefully planned with the quality and quantity of data in mind. Here are a few possibilities.

Advance Communication

There are essentially four times to communicate in advance of the survey actually arriving. The first is the early announcement that the survey will be conducted. For a given target audience, this may be the time that the sample from which the data will be collected has been identified. If the survey is related to evaluating a program that individuals are participating in, this is in advance of their participation. The early announcement contains the information about the survey, detailing the process, the rationale for responding, and how the data will be used.

A second opportunity is at the beginning of a formal process that is being studied. For example, in a business development conference that is being evaluated, this announcement would come at the opening of the conference. If it is a longitudinal study that includes routine data collection over a period of time regarding participation in, say, a master's degree program, the communication would come at the beginning of the program. This announcement in a formal setting provides the proper focus of attention on the data that are needed. It explains what is needed and the roles and responsibilities. It also explains how the survey results will be used and underscores what is in it for potential respondents. If copies of the results are to be distributed to respondents, it should be mentioned at this time. If actions will be taken to improve the program based on the results of the survey, it should be explained at this time.

A third opportunity for advance communication is at the end of a formal session. In an ideal setting, the questionnaire that will be sent a few weeks or months in the future is explained. For example, at the end of a business development conference, a sample of the participants is provided the questionnaire that will be sent in six months. A facilitator reviews the questionnaire in detail, explaining the type of data needed and if it is a complex questionnaire, perhaps providing an example. At the end of this discussion, a commitment is secured from the participants to provide the data. This step alone will often ensure that at least 10 to 15 percent of the responses are received. This is an excellent way to clarify any potential misunderstandings, to provide examples of what is needed, and to motivate the respondent to provide the data.

The final opportunity for advance communication is between the time of the formal process and the time the survey will be received. This is in an effort to keep the respondent focused, often reminding them what they should be accomplishing and the data they should be monitoring if appropriate. This keeps the commitment to provide data from fading from memory. Also, it keeps a dialogue going with respondents if the time frame between the launch of the project and the receipt of the survey is lengthy. Collectively, these time frames provide excellent opportunities for increasing the quality and quantity of the data.

Correspondence With the Survey

Almost every survey will have some kind of communiqué from an appropriate executive or administrator describing the survey and its importance. It is important for the person signing the correspondence to be the most influential individual possible to motivate the respondent. In some organizations, this is a top executive or CEO. For general population surveys, it could be an elected official. For nonprofits and NGOs, it should be the person whose name is most associated with the cause. For example, a memo introducing a survey to collect data regarding a particular charity is signed by a celebrity who has loaned her name to the organization to help build awareness.

The memo should briefly explain the purpose of the survey and how the data will be used. It should indicate what is in it for the respondent and for others, highlighting the need for accurate, complete, and timely data. Include the date by which the survey must be returned and, if feasible, the approximate date when the results will be made available. Finally, if possible, include in the memo the specific changes or improvements that will be made as a result of their input. This can be very powerful when participants think they can make a difference with their responses. The memo should end with, "Thank you in advance for responding," and indicate a point of contact.

Noted

Dillman, Smyth, and Christian describe three ways to encourage respondents to participate in your survey.

1. Establish trust.

2. Increase benefits of participation.

3. Decrease costs of participation.

Source: Dillman, Don A., Jolene D. Smyth, and Leah Melani Christian. (2009). *Internet, Mail, and Mixed-Mode Surveys: The Tailored Design Method,* 3rd edition. Hoboken, NJ: Wiley & Sons.

Instructions

Include a cover page on the survey with a list of instructions. These provide details about the mechanics and logistics of the survey, along with a point of contact for additional information. It is important for the respondents to understand who is sponsoring the study and ultimately how they will use the data. Instructions in addition to the introductory memo offer an opportunity to provide this information. They also offer an opportunity to show the reasons for participation, reminding the respondent once again why they should be involved and how their involvement will make a difference.

Include the due date and the time it will take for respondents to complete the survey. This is important because individuals often base their decision to respond on these expectations. It is not necessarily the number of pages that is important, but the time it will take to provide the data. This can be determined through pilot testing the questionnaire to secure an average time. To be accurate, the average time through pilot testing should be increased so respondents expect more time than completion requires. The goal is to have participants finish at or below the time stated to complete the survey.

A confidentiality statement is necessary. Some surveys are anonymous and the steps taken to retain anonymity should be described. However, in many cases, potential respondents do not necessarily believe anonymity exists, particularly for Internet-based surveys. Therefore, communicating confidentiality is critical. Specifics of who will see the raw data and the respondents' names should be provided, along with other steps you plan to take to maintain confidentiality. Finally, the return guidelines should be provided, indicating how the items should be submitted and any special instructions for submission.

Handling Special Issues

Sometimes, there are other correspondence issues that must be addressed. For example, if other individuals will be involved in providing correspondence either before or during the data collection, this should be carefully prepared, written, and coordinated so that all messages and instructions are consistent. If there are appropriate ads, media, or other communication, they should be highlighted within the memo and the instructions. They should be timely and consistent.

Occasionally, respondents will have questions about the purpose of the survey or specific content areas. It is important to include a point of contact to handle such questions. Sometimes, a detailed questionnaire may list multiple people to contact for questions. Figure 5-5 shows a checklist of action items regarding correspondence.

Basic Rule

Every type of survey should include contact information. The most accurate data come from participants who fully understand the survey, its purpose, and how the data they provide will be used. If respondents are unclear about anything, they should have a contact that can provide timely and concise clarification. This is an issue not to be overlooked when designing surveys and correspondence.

Figure 5-5. Checklist for Correspondence With Participants

☐ Send an early announcement when it's decided to perform the survey.

☐ Make an announcement at the beginning of the program.

☐ Make an announcement at the end of the formal program (copy of survey).

☐ Send "Keep them on task" memos.

☐ Send correspondence from others (sponsors, supporters, VIPs) when necessary.

☐ Send a memo with the survey.

☐ Include instructions for the survey.

☐ Include confidentiality statement.

☐ Clearly identify point of contact.

☐ Communicate the proper way to ask questions.

☐ Send first follow-up reminder.

☐ Send second follow-up reminder.

☐ Make an extra request for responses if necessary.

☐ Provide an incentive or gift for response.

☐ Send a summary of the survey results.

☐ Send a document detailing actions taken to improve the program.

Follow-Up Procedures

The follow-up procedures deserve special attention. Without the follow-up, response rates would be dramatically reduced (response rates are discussed in more detail in chapter 7). There are essentially four issues concerning follow-up methods.

Number

The number of follow-ups is important. Some surveys have only one carefully planned and orchestrated follow-up. This is best used for audiences who are very eager to respond but maybe need a subtle reminder. Some surveys may require several follow-ups or constant follow-ups until the appropriate amount of data has been obtained. Two follow-ups are generally recommended with the focus on providing a couple of reminders from different media, but not to bombard or harass the respondents.

Timing

The timing of follow-ups is based primarily on the audience. When sending a survey, include a return date. If the group of participants travel routinely, or potentially lack proper time to respond, the follow-up period may be as long as three weeks. For many potential respondents, the follow-up may be as little as one week. Depending on organization culture, length of the survey, and the motivation of the respondents, two weeks generally proves to be the best timing for a follow-up.

Type

The most important rule for delivering follow-up correspondence is to use a medium that is favored by the respondents, or a channel they appreciate. Since respondents may be motivated by different media, it is helpful to consider providing follow-ups in a different way than the questionnaire was administered. For example, if the questionnaire comes in an email, the follow-up might be a postcard. Although postcards aren't usually received anymore, they can be a novel way to draw attention to the survey. They can also attract the attention of those who might not be motivated by another email. A second reminder could be provided through a phone call. The phone call could be an attempt to try to connect with an individual, or a voicemail reminding them of the importance of the survey. Some survey respondents will have a voicemail scripted by a top executive. This will draw attention to the survey and hit the right button for some. The challenge is to pursue the different ways in which the respondent can be reached and then select the proper variety to make sure the message is received.

Content

The content of the message should follow some general guidelines. First, keep the message brief. After all, this is a follow-up. It is not intended to recite all the informa-

should emphasize the bene-
urn to responding, it should
ondents of any incentives or
The key is to make it short,

Processing

P01JDSURS

Liverpool John Moores University

Customer Number: 18589001	ISBN: 9781562868093
Budget/Fund Code	MGT1-2012
Classification	001.433
Loan Type/Stock	NONE
Site / Location	NONE
Shelfmark	001.433 PHI
Cutter 1	PHI
PL Category	General
Order Date	04/15/2013
Order Type	orders
PL Intellect. Level	Adult
Coutts shelfmark	Yes

Hand Notes:

LGUK002R001

are critical with any survey.
evidence must exist to show
data integrity. Here are a few
oroach to your survey design.

dentiality, specific steps that
led. This will require tracing
vill be communicated to the
ta and how the data will be
as access to the names of the

data can be a problem. This
fabricated. While this may be
few researchers, in a quest to
they are trying to prove. Also,
it of view. A very specific and
will go a long way in showing

Review and Use of the Results

A statement should be made about who will be allowed to view the results, when they will view them, and the rules under which the data will be viewed. A client or sponsor should have access to the data in advance to ensure there are no misunderstandings, particularly in the event clarification is needed. However, this review should not be a carte blanche opportunity to make adjustments or changes.

Perhaps the most important statement to make to participants is how the data will be used. It is imperative that process improvement, not performance evaluation, be of utmost importance in the use of the data. When the results of the survey are used to punish some particular group, the integrity of the study, the researchers, and even the sponsor will come into question. This is a sure way to guarantee that no additional data will be provided in the future from this particular group.

Finally, the storage of the data is important because sometimes the raw data storage can lead to leaks in the process. If you plan to destroy data, note it in the survey instructions, along with when it will be destroyed and who will destroy it. If you plan to store the data, a note about where it will be kept and how it will be protected should be provided.

Tracking Returns

It is important to have quick tabulation of the data. If the survey is electronic, this step is generally easy. If it is paper-based, the task is obviously more difficult. The faster the data are analyzed and progress is reported, the faster the problems can be identified. When the data show low response, this may trigger additional follow-ups in particular areas. It may mean that others need to get involved. Additional correspondence may be required to keep the project on task. Sometimes a low response rate is a result of a misunderstanding or misinterpretation about the survey itself. On occasion, a competitive spirit can be generated as respondents in one area seem to exceed those in others. The key is to tabulate quickly, report results quickly, and make adjustments as needed to keep the data flowing.

Tracking Costs

The costs of the survey or questionnaire should be monitored closely for two important reasons. First, in the spirit of accountability, costs should be monitored and categorized into different data sets. This allows researchers to clearly show the funding sources where the money went, perhaps in the context of budget and cost requirements. The other reason is that sometimes surveys are used to collect data for projects being evaluated up to ROI. This requires that full costs of the project or program be incorporated, including the cost of evaluation. When this is the case, all of the costs must be included. These generally include the categories shown in Figure 5-6.

Figure 5-6. Tracking the Costs of a Survey

Categories for Tracking Costs
1. Materials
2. Fees and postage
3. Technology and software use
4. Time of researchers
5. Time of others supporting the survey project
6. Time of responders, if appropriate
7. Contract services
8. Preparation and skill building

Validity and Reliability

A final step in designing your survey instrument is ensuring its validity and reliability. Accuracy of the questionnaire involves confirming that needed content is included, the right questions are asked the right way, and the instructions and supporting information are included. The validity and reliability of the instrument should be reviewed during the pilot. To be an effective data collection instrument, the survey should provide consistent results over time (reliability) and measure what it is intended to measure (validity).

Validity

Validity is probably the most important characteristic of a survey instrument. A valid survey instrument measures what it is intended to measure based on the research objectives. The degree to which the survey instrument performs this function satisfactorily is usually called the relative validity. Four types of validity are 1) content, 2) predictive, 3) construct, and 4) concurrent.

Content validity refers to the extent to which an instrument measures all facets of the research objectives. To ensure you cover all content, refer to your objectives map (chapter 2) and use the specific measures for each research objective as the basis for the questions. Additionally, create a survey map. To create a survey map, list the survey objectives in the left-hand column of a table, and the item number in the right-hand column. Table 5-1 presents a survey map for the International Car Rental survey found in chapter 8, Table 8-6.

Table 5-1. Survey Map

Survey Map

Objectives	Survey Questions
1. Participants will complete course requirements.	Q2
2. Participants will rate the program as relevant to their jobs.	Q3, Q4, Q5, Q6, Q8
3. Participants will rate the program as important to their jobs.	Q7
4. Participants will indicate opportunities for improving the course.	Q42
5. Participants must demonstrate acceptable performance on each major competency.	Q9, Q10, Q11
6. Participants will routinely use the competencies with team members.	Q12, Q13, Q14, Q16, Q17, Q18
7(a) Participants will report barriers to successful application of the leadership competencies.	Q15, Q19, Q20
7(b) Participants will report enablers to successful application of the leadership competencies.	Q15, Q21, Q22
8(a) Participants and team members will drive improvements in at least two business measures due to the course, resulting in either profit, cost savings, or cost avoidance.	Q23, Q24, Q25, Q26, Q27, Q28, Q29, Q30, Q1
8(b) Participants and team members will drive improvements in at least two business measures due to the course, resulting in either profit, cost savings, or cost avoidance.	Q31, Q32, Q33, Q34, Q35, Q36, Q37, Q38, Q1
9. Participants will identify additional benefits.	Q39
*Cost data required by ROI analysis plan	Q40, Q41

Predictive validity, also known as criterion validity, refers to the extent to which scores on a survey instrument can predict future behaviors or results. For example, a survey instrument used to assess new employees that successfully predicts their performance on the job is an instrument with predictive validity.

Construct validity refers to the extent to which an instrument represents the construct it purports to measure. A construct is an abstract variable, such as the skill, attitude, or ability that the instrument is intended to measure. Examples of constructs are:

▶ attitude toward supervisor

- ability to read a scale
- skill in conducting an effective performance discussion.

As a first step in defending construct validity, define all parts of the construct and make a case to show that the survey is an adequate measure of that construct. Following the guidance in chapter 2 will ensure you take this step. Then defend construct validity using one or more techniques such as:

- expert opinion
- correlations
- logical deductions
- criterion group studies.

Concurrent validity refers to the extent to which an instrument agrees with the results of other instruments administered at approximately the same time to measure the same characteristics.

Strategies for improving validity include:

- Content experts review each survey item.
- Check for even and consistent representation of survey objectives.
- Include an appropriate number of items given your research objectives.
- Take steps to reduce potential response bias.
- Administer objectively.

Reliability

Reliability is another important characteristic of a survey instrument. A reliable survey is one that is consistent enough that subsequent measurements of an item give approximately the same results. Several procedures that can help ensure a survey is reliable are 1) test/retest, 2) alternate-form method, 3) internal consistency reliability, 4) inter-rater reliability.

Test/retest involves administering the survey to the same group of employees at two different time periods and calculating the correlation of the scores. If there is a high degree of positive correlation, the test is reliable.

Alternate-form method, also known as parallel-forms, involves constructing two similar instruments and administering those to employees at the same time, and analyzing the correlation between the two scores. If there is a high positive correlation, the instrument is considered to be reliable. Constructing a similar instrument is time consuming, which may make this approach impractical.

There are several forms of internal consistency reliability. Internal consistency reliability measures the consistency of question items that reflect the same construct and yield the same results. Two specific forms of internal consistency reliability are split-half reliability and inter-item reliability. Split-half reliability involves splitting the survey into two equal parts and comparing the results. For example, it might be appropriate to compare the even-numbered questions with the odd-numbered questions. The scores of the two halves are compared, and their correlations are checked. Once again, a high correlation indicates a reliable instrument. Inter-item correlations compares correlations between all pairs of questions that test the same construct by calculating the mean of all paired correlations. It is a procedure in which correlations are calculated among each of the items on the survey.

Last, inter-rater reliability applies to surveys requiring the collection of data by individual observers. Also known as inter-observer reliability, here we test to ensure that the observers are consistent in their scoring. For example, if you are scoring call center representatives and their performance in dealing with customers, observers would use a survey instrument to check off their performance based on categories. In this case, you would calculate the percent of agreement between the raters for each category. If the survey includes an actual numerical scale rather than a categorical scale, you would determine the correlations between the ratings to estimate the reliability between the scores.

Some tips to help ensure you develop a reliable instrument include:
▶ Provide clear and consistent instructions for the survey.
▶ Ensure sufficient time for responses.
▶ Ensure the same amount of time for responses.
▶ Ensure consistency in all steps and procedures.
▶ Use an adequate number of items for each research objective.

How do validity and reliability relate to each other? It is often said that if a survey instrument is truly valid, it is also reliable. However, if an instrument is reliable, it may not always be valid. Table 5-2 demonstrates the relationship between validity and reliability. While extensive amounts of time and testing can go into ensuring a valid and reliable instrument, it is important to always balance how much you spend on survey development with the value of the survey itself.

Table 5-2. Relationship Between Validity and Reliability

		Reliable?	
		Yes	No
Valid?	No	Undesirable	Worst Case
	Yes	Ideal	Not Possible

Getting It Done

Now that you have been introduced to the basics of survey instrument design for the best response rate, consider your last survey. Does it have a professional layout? Is there a logical flow of questions? Based on the specific questions, were data easy to tabulate? When communicating the survey to respondents, did you include multiple touch points? Did you deliver the communication via multiple channels?

Response Rates

What's Inside This Chapter

Whether you administer your survey to the entire population or to only a sample, without response, you have no information. After reading this chapter, you will be able to:

▶ Avoid asking for too much detail, which can negatively affect the response rate
▶ Approach survey design and administration with maximum response in mind
▶ Use proven techniques to ensure a successful response rate
▶ Create the environment, climate, commitment, and motivation that support involvement in survey projects

Why This Is Important

Response rates are important in survey design and analysis, and low response rates always raise concerns. If the response rates are too low, useable information will be negligible.

Response rate is different from sample size, as discussed in the previous chapter. Sample size represents an appropriate-sized portion of the population, from whom we can collect data and make inferences to the larger population. Response rate refers to the number of surveys actually received. If the number received does not represent the appropriate sample size, inferences to the population cannot be made with the level of accuracy and confidence planned. This poses a challenge, particularly for large population studies.

Think About This

Assume you have a population of 20,000 to whom you want to make an inference regarding the population's attitude about a new incentive plan. However, you only want to gather data from a sample rather than surveying everyone in the population. Using your knowledge of sampling, you determine that responses from 377 people will provide a good indication of what the total population thinks about the plan.

To ensure you gather data from the entire 377, you will likely have to administer the survey to a larger number of people. The question is, "What is the number?" To answer the question, solve for the following:

$$N = \frac{s}{r}$$

N = number of surveys to administer

s = target sample size

r = estimated response rate given the audience

If: s = 377 and r = .50

Then: $N = \frac{377}{.50} = 754$

This tells you that you must administer the survey to 754 people to ensure responses from the 377 sample, based on an estimated 50 percent response rate.

For many surveys, particularly when evaluating programs, sampling is not appropriate. This means that you ultimately survey the entire population and without appropriate response, your results will be skewed, based on non-response. For example, when administering a survey to capture data describing the extent to which business measures improve as a result of a program, inference is not made to non-respondents. Therefore, the benefits of the program only represent benefits of those who respond. This no-data-no-improvement standard ensures program benefits are never overstated (Phillips and Stawarkski, 2008). To take this a step further, assume you are going to convert those benefits to monetary value and compare them to the cost of the program. A standard in calculating the ROI of a program requires that the evaluator account for fully-loaded costs (Phillips and Phillips, 2008). This means if you train 100 people and 50 respond with program benefits, you only capture the benefits from the 50, but you capture the costs of all 100. This lack of response could easily affect your ROI to the point that it drives it negative. This is an incentive to ensure you get an appropriate response rate. How you do this depends on the extent to which you employ the strategies in this chapter.

Communication Issues

The first set of actions for improving response rates focuses on the communication between the study organizers and the participants. Communication begins early and often throughout the process, providing as much detail as possible and creating a rationale for responding.

Provide Advance Communication

Advance communication is always critical. It sets expectations for the survey and response. For example, in a follow-up evaluation for ASTD's annual International Conference & Exposition, participants in the selected sample group were notified in advance of their participation in the survey. Individuals were randomly invited to be a part of the sample, and were removed from the survey at their choosing. If their responses were not received within one week, they were replaced in the sample. This selection process ensured that every person in the sample was committed to provide follow-up data. This advance communication removes the surprise element and lowers the resistance to providing the data.

Communicate the Purpose

Make sure that participants understand the reason for the survey, including who or what has initiated it and how the data will be used. Participants should know whether the survey is the result of an ongoing systematic process or part of a special project. If the questionnaire is anonymous, communicate clearly to participants the steps that will be taken to ensure anonymity. Research has shown that the most important word to use when influencing people to respond is "because."

When surveying the employees of a midsized non-governmental organization to evaluate the effectiveness of the performance management system, the purpose of the survey was clearly described. The survey was intended to review the performance management system and secure input for changes, with a promise of adjustments to the program to make it an efficient and effective tool. This effort contributed to the 80 percent response rate. The employees became interested in participating when they understood the reasons behind the survey.

Identify Who Will See the Results

Respondents need to know who will see the data and the results of the questionnaire. If the questionnaire is confidential, it should clearly be communicated to participants that no comments or feedback will be linked to respondents' names. If senior executives will see results in aggregate, the respondents should know. Provide as much detail as possible about who will receive the data, when, and for what purpose.

A survey of employees in a large county in California was administered to review the success of the employee assistance program. As part of the announcement, the study organizers indicated that the county commissioners would be personally reviewing results of the study in a planned meeting on a particular named date. This specific detail encouraged some people to voice their concerns about this employee benefit to those commissioners, resulting in a 78 percent response rate.

Describe the Data Integration Process

When using multiple types of surveys (such as self-administered questionnaires, interviews, focus groups), explain to respondents how you plan to combine data. They should know how the data are weighted and how they will be integrated into the final reporting.

In a survey of the effectiveness of a management development center used by three Rome-based agencies, participants and their managers were told that data would be collected with questionnaires, focus groups, and one-on-one interviews. The specific number involved in each method was outlined in the notifying memorandum, with an explanation of how the data would be integrated. The letter stated that the interviews provided the agenda for the focus groups and identified the issues to address in the questionnaires. The focus groups provided qualitative data to be combined with the qualitative data provided in the questionnaire. This technical detail reassured all participants that the data collected would be used, and in what manner.

Let Participants Know They Are Part of a Sample

For large programs, you may use a sampling process to identify respondents. When that is the case, explain to respondents that they are part of a carefully selected sample and that their input will be used to make decisions regarding a much larger target audience. This action often appeals to a sense of responsibility for participants to provide useable, accurate data for the questionnaire.

Middle-level executives at a large Canadian bank were involved in a pilot of an expensive and comprehensive executive leadership program. An evaluation was undertaken to gauge the value of the program. Participants were told that their input would determine the fate of the program. This prompted complete participation.

Add Emotional Appeal

It could be very helpful to add an element of emotional appeal, if possible. This involves connecting the audience to an issue of importance that could trigger a little more emotion than a simple request for response. For example, the chief financial officer (CFO) for one of the largest consulting companies sent a memo to a sample group involved in implementing a sales platform. Here is what the CFO stated in the memo:

"We know that you are interested in a system-wide implementation of this new sales platform, but to do so with all 100,000 consultants is a tremendous expenditure. We piloted this project with 120 consultants and you are part of the group. Because we are asking for actual impact data and the extent to which this new platform has influenced your sales data, we need your direct input.

"If we do not hear from you, we will assume that you have seen no improvement. You are voting on this new sales platform, and if you think it should be implemented with or without adjustments, please complete the questionnaire. This will be your 'yes' vote. If you think the platform should not be implemented, you can vote 'no' by ignoring the questionnaire and we will record you as having no value connected to this new platform."

This communication brings a new dimension to the situation. A consultant may not want to respond for a variety of reasons, yet would like the implementation of this new platform to move forward. He now realizes response is necessary to ensure that his vote is counted.

Design Issues

As mentioned in chapter 5, the design of the survey instrument is an important part of the response rate issue. An improperly designed survey instrument makes it easy to ignore the questionnaire. Several design issues can help spark attention and secure the response needed.

Design for Simplicity

While a simple questionnaire may not provide the full scope of data necessary for a comprehensive analysis, the simplified approach should be followed when questions are developed and the total scope of the questionnaire is finalized. Every effort should be made to keep it as brief as possible. Unnecessary questions should be omitted. If an issue will not be "acted on," maybe the question should not be asked.

Basic Rule

If you do not plan to use the data, do not ask the question.

Keep It Professional

While it should not be a concern in most organizations, unfortunately there are too many cases where a questionnaire does not appear professional. It may be thrown together using a generic template or include meaningless clip art. Respondents must respect the survey; otherwise they will merely go through the motions of responding, if they respond at all.

Think About This

An attractive format, an engaging font, a professional appearance, and easy-to-follow steps will help to get the participant involved. Meaningful graphics and colors may also help.

Use Local Management Support

Management involvement at the local level is critical for response-rate success. Managers can distribute the questionnaires themselves, make reference to the questionnaire in meetings, follow up to see whether employees have completed their questionnaires, and generally show support for completing the questionnaire.

In a survey of employees on the effectiveness of a customer service initiative at a large telecommunications company, an anonymous questionnaire was provided to department managers to distribute to targeted employees. An envelope was also provided, with a request to seal the completed questionnaire for the department manager to collect and send to the survey team. This element of local management involvement added a new dimension to the questionnaire. The manager is now the person waiting on the questionnaire, thus placing more obligation on the participant to respond. Although the survey was anonymous, 98 percent of the questionnaires were returned, using local management support.

Build on Earlier Data

Data are sometimes collected sequentially. In an evaluation of a learning and development program, for example, participants often provide reaction and learning data, and follow-up data are collected three or four months later. To secure commitment to evaluate a leadership development program in an electric utility cooperative, the participants provided reaction and learning data during the program, and were committed to provide more data at a later date. In the follow-up, they were reminded of the earlier results and their commitment to respond to the follow-up questionnaire. This formed the bridge between the data previously provided, and connected it to the next set. They were now more involved, more so than when they provided the earlier data. Research supports the theory that if small steps or progress can be made with participants, the more likely they are to continue with a project in the ensuing follow-up.

Basic Rule

Remind participants of their commitment to the project.

Pilot Test the Questionnaire

Consider conducting a pilot test on a sample of the target audience. A pilot test is one of the best ways to ensure that a survey is designed properly and that the questions flow adequately. Pilot testing can be accomplished quickly with a very small sample and can reveal problems with a questionnaire before it is administered to the target audience. This will alleviate potential confusion, which sometimes negatively influences participants' willingness to respond.

For example, in a survey for the designers of a tractor and equipment manufacturing company, three product designers were asked to complete the questionnaire and provide feedback. These individuals were readily available and were representative members of the target audience. They knew the context well enough to sort through the questionnaire. During the pilot, the timing of completing the questionnaire was recorded to determine the duration, and they were asked how each question could be changed or modified to be worded more clearly. Finally, they were asked to indicate a better way to explore the issues they needed and if there were any changes to the questionnaire they felt would be necessary. These designers, in a very small group experiment, made a significant difference in the questionnaire.

Rewards and Responsibilities

Sometimes it is helpful to clearly show "what is in it" for the individual respondent. Using a variety of rewards, both tangible and intangible, can create desire among some individuals. Still others need to be reminded of their particular responsibilities, suggesting certain consequences if they do not meet them or ignore the issue altogether. When combined, these are powerful tools to increase response rates.

Recognize the Expertise of Participants

It is sometimes helpful to recognize the expertise of the audience. After all, the individuals being surveyed must have some expertise, or they would lack credibility to respond. Reminding them that they are experts elevates them to the most credible source status, and tells them they are experts in the precise types of data needed. It is helpful to let them *know* that they are the experts.

For example, in measuring the success of product training in a large financial services firm, the customer service representatives in the branches were asked to indicate the extent to which the program had actually improved sales of a particular product. They were sent the questionnaire with these comments:

"We need feedback based on your expertise. We need to know the extent to which this program has helped you sell this product. You are the most credible person to provide this information. No one else can provide accurate data. You are the expert. We need your input and five minutes of your time."

This clearly labels these respondents as experts. Important research has substantiated that labeling people properly and positioning them as experts can make a difference in their involvement and response rates.

Consider the Use of Incentives

A variety of incentives to complete questionnaires can be offered, and they can usually be grouped into three categories.

A first category is for incentives provided in exchange for the completed questionnaire. For example, when respondents return the questionnaire, they will receive a small gift, such as an iPod Shuffle, book, coffee mug, or umbrella. If identity is an issue, a neutral third party can collect the questionnaires, and the respondent can advise the study coordinator that the questionnaire has been sent. The gift is then sent to the respondent.

For example, in a follow-up study of ASTD's annual conference, participants were provided a copy of one of ASTD's bestselling books in exchange for returning the completed questionnaire. The participants were told that their names did not have to be included on the questionnaire. The survey team requested that the participants inform them when the questionnaire was completed so that they could send the book of their choice. This exchange of questionnaire-for-book connected to the audience because they could select a very popular book according to each individual's interest or field.

A second category of incentive includes those that make participants feel guilty about not responding. Examples include money clipped to the questionnaire, a coupon for lunch or a beverage, or a pen enclosed in the envelope. Respondents are asked to "take the money, buy a cup of coffee or tea, and fill out the questionnaire."

In a follow-up study of a new software system at the headquarters of a large pharmaceutical company, the participants were provided a $5 coupon to be redeemed at the cafeteria for completing a 10-minute questionnaire. The feeling was that the participants would experience some guilt if they used the coupon without completing the questionnaire. Although this seems minor, it influences some people to the point where they will complete the questionnaire.

A third category of incentives is designed to obtain a quick response. This approach is based on the assumption that a quick response will ensure a greater response rate. If an individual delays completing the questionnaire, the odds of ever completing it diminish considerably. The initial group of respondents may receive a more expensive gift or they may be part of a drawing for an incentive.

In a study of a management development program at the Department of Defense agency, the respondents were provided an opportunity to win a prize. The first 25 participants responding would have their names entered in a drawing for a parking spot in the senior executive space, free for one month. In that particular agency, offering a high 1-in-25 chance of winning the free spot was a powerful and meaningful incentive. This type of incentive will trigger an excellent response rate almost every time.

In another example, family practice physicians were sent a survey from a medical malpractice insurance company. The first 50 responding were offered an entry for a drawing for a $500 American Express gift certificate, a 1-in-50 chance of winning. The next 50 were offered an opportunity in a drawing for another $500 gift certificate, giving a chance of 1 in 99 for the second draw. In essence, the first group received two chances of winning. The study organizers were surprised to receive 300 questionnaires within a two-day timeframe, motivated principally by this early-response incentive.

Have an Executive Sign the Introductory Letter

Respondents are always interested in who sent the letter with the questionnaire. For maximum effectiveness, a senior executive who is responsible for the area where the participants are employed should sign the letter. The employees may be more willing to respond to a senior executive when compared to situations in which a member of the program team signs the letter. The same concept works for public and community surveys. A signature from the mayor, governor, or community leader can spark a response.

Send Results to the Participants

Respondents should see the results of the questionnaire. More importantly, participants should understand that they will receive copies of the study (at least in a summary form) as they are asked to provide the data. Following through on the promise will influence response rates for future evaluations.

In a survey of high school principals in a large educational district in Texas, the data were immediately summarized and returned to the audience. This was accomplished at a predetermined time, two weeks after the close of the surveys, and was announced in the questionnaire. Because the principals wanted to see others' comments about the particular issues, a 77 percent response rate was achieved.

Report on the Use of Results

In addition to showing the respondents the summary of the data received, it is helpful to show them how the data were used. Respondents like to know that they will make a difference, and their biggest concern is often that the questionnaire data will be either not read or not used, at least in the manner in which it should be. Precisely showing the actions taken provides some assurance that their participation will make a difference.

The survey feedback action loop, shown in Figure 6-1, is an important part of data collection. Survey participants provide feedback on the results, and action is taken as a result of that feedback. Reporting results and the corresponding actions taken completes the cycle to enhance response rates in the future. This sometimes helps to build a culture of accountability between researchers and the audiences. If that culture does not exist, it is helpful to be precise about when the data concerning the actions taken will be provided.

In an association survey to chapter leaders concerning the relationship between the headquarters and chapters, the results were sent to participants within two weeks of the data collection and the actions taken as a result of the survey were detailed three weeks later. This was communicated in a letter with the original questionnaire, using a timeline to indicate when the data would be due, when they would be analyzed, when the results would be sent, and when the identified action items would be forwarded. These actions helped to secure a 92 percent response rate.

Figure 6-1. Survey Feedback Action Loop

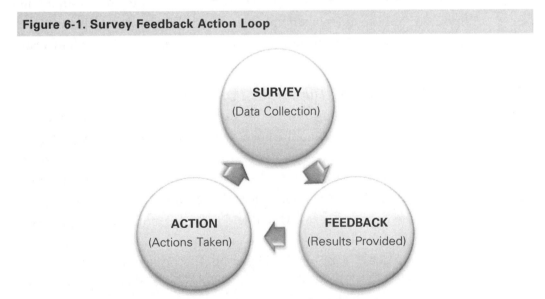

Provide an Update to Create Pressure

In some cases, it may be appropriate to provide an update on current response totals and the progress of the evaluation project. If individuals understand how others are doing and how many responses have been returned, they may feel subtle pressure and be reminded to provide data by completing their questionnaire. When several groups are involved, a competitive spirit is created, placing increased pressure to respond.

In a survey of insurance agents addressing how well they have used the tools and processes from a business development conference, the early response results were reported in different regions to show a running percentage total that was updated daily. This triggered the district directors to write notes encouraging the agents to participate and provide the data. This competitive spirit not only improved the response rates, but sparked district managers' interest in providing personal follow-up.

Present Previous Response Rates

Sometimes a survey has been conducted previously, with the same or similar group or in another organization evaluating the same project or program. When this is the case, building on earlier results can be helpful. In this case, participants are provided data on previous successful response rates, thus creating an expectation for the new group.

In a follow-up study of account representatives for a financial services firm, the previous data about the same type of project was described. The participants were told that earlier evaluations of this particular system yielded a response rate of over 85 percent, and at least that level of response was expected from this group. This placed additional emphasis on responding, yielding a 98 percent response rate. Significant research supports that the technique of providing earlier data will increase the level of response.

Introduce the Questionnaire During the Program

Sometimes, it is helpful to explain to the respondents and other key stakeholders in an earlier meeting that they will be required or asked to provide certain types of data. When this is feasible, questionnaires should be reviewed, question-by-question, so that the respondents understand the purpose and issues, and know how to respond. Although the questionnaire will be sent later, (for example, within three to six months), the respondents see what is involved and make a commitment to respond.

In an evaluation of a leadership development program for a rental car company, participants were provided a copy of the follow-up questionnaire at the end of a five-day program. In a 20-minute session, the facilitator reviewed each question and provided an example. Four months later, the questionnaire was sent. This technique helped to produce an 81 percent response rate.

Administrative Issues

The administration of the data collection process is important to response rate, and involves a variety of logistical and administrative details. When addressed properly, these details can increase the ease of responding. Ignoring them can make it easy to forget to respond.

Use Follow-Up Reminders

Send a follow-up reminder one week after participants receive the questionnaire and another reminder two weeks after the questionnaire is received. In some situations, a third follow-up is recommended.

Noted

Sometimes, it is effective to send the follow-ups through different media. For example, a questionnaire might be sent through the regular mail, the first follow-up reminder might be a telephone call, and a second follow-up reminder might be sent through email.

In a large financial services firm, the commercial loan officers were involved in a program on negotiating large projects. In a follow-up survey regarding the effectiveness of the program, the participants received a questionnaire and two follow-up reminders. One follow-up reminder was actually a phone call from the facilitator, who was a well-respected expert in the field and an author of several books. The follow-up reminder had this script:

"We know that you enjoyed the program and found it to be valuable. You have indicated this in your feedback, but the proof of our efforts will lie in the difference the program makes in your work—the success you enjoy with your negotiations. To determine that, we need the information on the questionnaire you received last week. Take a few minutes of your time to provide the data so we will know how much improvement has been made."

This reminder appealed to the individual providing the reminder because it represented a different medium than the one they chose for the questionnaire.

Consider a Captive Audience

The best way to obtain a high response rate is to collect data from a captive audience. As part of a program follow-up session, a routine meeting, or a mandatory session designed for data collection, participants are asked to provide input, usually during the first few minutes of the meeting. Sometimes, a routine meeting (such as a weekly sales meeting or staff meeting) provides the perfect setting for collecting data. This approach is ideal in a major program with a series of meetings; in that case, each subsequent meeting is an opportunity to collect data about the previous one.

In an office products firm, the quarterly sales meeting provided the sales reps an excellent opportunity for follow-up. Tools were provided containing specific instructions and details on their use. Their reaction and learning about the tools were collected at that meeting, and at the next meeting three months later, the sales team provided data about the success with application and impact. They were reminded about this in several ways, and generous examples of how to provide the data were given. The important point is that the data were collected from a captive audience, ensuring a 100 percent response rate, as all individuals were provided time in the meeting to complete the questionnaire and place it in a box as they left the meeting.

Select the Appropriate Medium for Easy Response

The response should be as easy as possible. It is important that the medium of the questionnaire (paper, web, or email) matches the culture of the participants. The medium should be selected for the convenience of the respondents, not the evaluator. Sometimes, an optional response medium can be offered in order to make responding more convenient for some participants.

These days, the use of more personal communication devices can present an ideal scenario for follow-up questionnaires. One organization was interested in knowing the value of the new tools provided to the team as part of a knowledge management system. The group was provided a text message which required a three-minute response, maximum. This particular medium fit the audience and yielded a 94 percent response rate.

Estimate the Necessary Time to Complete the Questionnaire

Respondents often have a concern about the time necessary to complete the questionnaire. A very lengthy questionnaire may quickly turn off the respondents and cause them to discard it. Sometimes, lengthy questionnaires can be completed quickly because of many forced-choice questions or statements that make responding easier. However, the number of pages may frighten the respondent. Therefore, indicating the estimated length of time needed to complete the questionnaire—in the letter or noted in the communication—is helpful. A word of caution is necessary, however. The amount of time must be realistic. Purposely underestimating it can do more harm than good.

Show the Timing of the Planned Steps

Sometimes, the respondents want to know more detail regarding when they can see the results or when the results will be presented to particular groups. A timeline should be presented, showing when different phases of the process occur—such as when to respond, when the data will be analyzed, when the data will be presented to different groups, and when the results will be returned to the respondents in a summary report. The timetable must be followed to maintain the confidence and trust of the individuals.

A survey was taken in a state police department to judge the success of a new ethics policy. Because the issue was controversial and there was a lack of trust between the administration and the police officers, it was important to show that senior leaders were serious about this survey. The survey indicated a timeline of when milestones would occur and what would be seen. The dates for the survey to be returned were indicated, along with the dates that analysis would be completed and when the data summary would be available for viewing on a particular website. They even provided the actual times of day that the data would be available (follow-up included an email summary to each of the precinct offices). The police officers were told that the necessary changes based on the survey would be made at the next commissioner's meeting, and that every item cited would be explained in terms of the action taken or not taken, with rationale. The actual date of the commissioner's meeting was provided, along with the time that the actions and related information would be available, up to the minute on the website, followed up on the same day with a summarized copy. This precise timing of the steps provided some assurance that actions would be taken, and accountability would be in place to enforce the suggestions made in the memorandum.

Personalize the Process

Participants usually respond well to personal messages and requests. Personalize the letter accompanying the questionnaire, if possible. In addition, if it is possible, use personal phone calls to deliver follow-up reminders. Calls may be made by the program facilitator, a manager, an executive, or even the expert in the field being introduced to participants. A personal touch brings sincerity and a sense of responsibility to the process. It also further encourages participants to respond by explaining to them the importance of their data.

In a survey of the Fortune 500 top executives, the ROI Institute wrote personal notes to each survey recipient. With 49 of the organizations eliminated from the initial analysis, 451 surveys were sent and 451 personal notes were written. The notes connected the survey to the organization, stating, "We are a subcontractor, a loyal customer, a fan, an investor." Any personal connection was made in the most attractive and credible way possible. The personal note was written directly on the paper-based survey, which probably helped the response rate significantly. Research shows that personal notes written on the survey reap dramatic improvement and response rates.

Collect Data Anonymously or Confidentially

Respondents are more likely to provide frank and candid feedback if their names are not on the questionnaires, particularly when the program is going astray or is off-target. Every effort should be made to protect the anonymous input, and explanations should be provided as to how the data are analyzed, minimizing the demographic makeup of respondents so that the individuals cannot be identified in the analysis. Confidentiality means that data sources are protected along with their linkage to data.

Chapter Summary

Collectively, these techniques help boost response rates of follow-up questionnaires. Using all these strategies can result in a 60 to 90 percent response rate, even with lengthy questionnaires that might take 30 minutes to complete. To achieve your desired response rate requires determination, focus, and discipline. Figure 6-2 shows this concept.

Figure 6-2. Response Rate Strategy

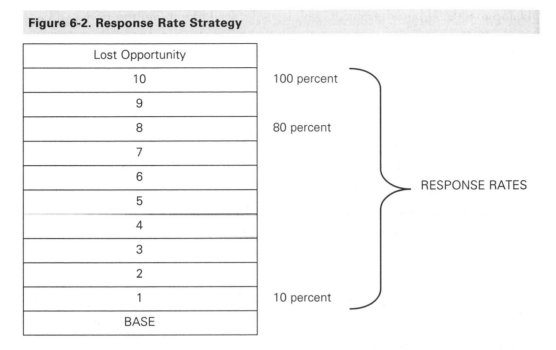

If surveys or questionnaires are distributed with little or no effort to increase response rate, there will be a very low response level. This approach will usually generate a 10 percent or less response rate, inadequate for most survey processes. When specific techniques are used, each technique yields a few more responses. Some are very powerful for a particular group, while others are less powerful. Each layer adds responses. It is suggested that at least 10 or more techniques outlined in this chapter be used to improve the response rate (see Table 6-1 for a checklist of techniques). Response rates can be improved when there is a deliberate approach, essentially distinguishing this type of follow-up from the deluge of questionnaires and surveys routinely received by the target audience. Many, if not most, of the routine ones are quickly deleted or ignored. This survey must be presented differently to elicit different results.

Too often, not enough effort is put into planning for a successful response rate. Unfortunately, without responses, there are no data; therefore, there is no information.

Table 6.1. Techniques to Increase Response Rates

1. Provide advance communication. ☐
2. Communicate the purpose. ☐
3. Identify who will see the results. ☐
4. Describe the data integration process. ☐
5. Let the target audience know that they are part of a sample. ☐
6. Add emotional appeal. ☐
7. Design for simplicity. ☐
8. Make it look professional and attractive. ☐
9. Use the local manager support. ☐
10. Build on earlier data. ☐
11. Pilot test the questionnaire. ☐
12. Recognize the expertise of participants. ☐
13. Consider the use of incentives. ☐
14. Have an executive sign the introductory letter. ☐
15. Send a copy of the results to the participants. ☐
16. Report the use of results. ☐
17. Provide an update to create pressure to respond. ☐
18. Present previous responses. ☐
19. Introduce the questionnaire during the program. ☐
20. Use follow-up reminders. ☐
21. Consider a captive audience. ☐
22. Consider the appropriate medium for easy response. ☐
23. Estimate the necessary time to complete the questionnaire. ☐
24. Show the timing of the planned steps. ☐
25. Personalize the process. ☐
26. Collect data anonymously or confidentially. ☐

Getting It Done

Consider an upcoming survey project. Plan for a successful response by completing the table below.

Plan for High Response

What can I do **before** administering the survey?

What can I do **during** the response period?

What can I do **after** receiving responses to the survey?

Data Summary and Reporting

▪▪

What's Inside This Chapter

This chapter presents some of the basic concepts to help get you started summarizing and reporting your results. After reading this chapter, you will be able to:

▶ Distinguish between the levels of measurement
▶ Apply basic descriptive statistics
▶ Describe three basic statistical tests
▶ Describe key issues in developing your report

Levels of Measurement

With data in hand, it is now time to analyze results. There are many resources available to provide you technical details on how to analyze data most appropriately, given the measures you take.

As you know, a survey can include a variety of types of questions. Each type of question presents an analysis opportunity. Not to be confused with the four- and five-level evaluation frameworks (Kirkpatrick, 1998; Phillips, 1983), the levels of measurement refer to the classification of measurement scales developed by psychologist Stanley Smith Stevens (1946). Stevens' theory suggests that measurement be classified in four categories: nominal, ordinal, interval, and ratio.

Noted

Researchers debate the merit of Stevens' measurement classification scheme. While the levels of measurement are widely adopted, they are not necessarily universally accepted.

Nominal Scale

Nominal scales are those scales for which the response choice is simply a category that has the same value of all other categories on the scale. Nominal or categorical measures are discrete and have no numeric value. They represent a "check the box" type of response. Analysis includes counting the number of responses for each response choice, but it does not include mathematical computations such as addition, subtraction, multiplication, and division. An example of a survey question based on a nominal scale is shown in Table 7-1.

Table 7-1. Example of Nominal Scale

In what region of the country do you work?

☐ North

☐ South

☐ East

☐ West

Ordinal Scale

Ordinal scales are rank-ordered groupings along one dimension. Responses to these types of questions represent the number in order of priority, preference, or performance of a set of categorical choices. The distances between the choices have no meaning. For example, in a speed-walking race, the results would be categorized as first, second, or third place. Each category represents a position in terms of completing the race, but the ranking is not based on a numerical value of distance between the person who ranked first, second, or third.

A requirement when using this level of measurement is that the relationship between choices must be such that each choice represents a higher level of preference, priority, or performance. Armstrong's (1974) axiom of transitivity required for ordinal level of measurement states that if choice A is greater than choice B, and choice B is greater than choice C, then choice A is greater than choice C, or:

$$\text{If } (A>B) \text{ and } (B>C), \text{ then } (A>C)$$

The classic Likert-type ordinal scale meets Armstrong's criteria where respondents might choose from options "very satisfied," "satisfied," "neutral," "dissatisfied," or "very dissatisfied." A choice of "very satisfied" is greater (or more satisfied) than a choice of "satisfied"; "satisfied" is greater than "dissatisfied"; "dissatisfied" is greater than "very dissatisfied"; therefore, "very satisfied" is greater than "very dissatisfied." So the order of and progression toward (or away from) satisfaction is evident; however, the difference between one choice of satisfaction and another is unknown. Therefore, with ordinal scales, we can identify order, but not the numerical difference in the order.

Because ordinal measures are discrete and have no numerical value, the arithmetic operations available are limited, as in the case of nominal measures. Like nominal data, ordinal data are counted; however, with ordinal data we can put responses into "order" based on priority, preference, or performance, whereas with nominal data we cannot. Table 7-2 shows two examples of survey questions representing the ordinal level of measurement.

Noted

Both nominal and ordinal levels of measurement are considered categorical data. They can be numeric or non-numeric. While appropriate statistical analysis can be applied to these data, response choices are considered qualitative.

Table 7-2. Examples of Ordinal Scales

Please rank the following tools in terms of usefulness to you when you travel for work. (1=Most Useful; 4=Least Useful)

___ Dropbox

___ Evernote

___ Skype

___ iCloud

Given the tool you selected as most useful to you when you travel for work, how satisfied are you with its reliability?

Very Dissatisfied	Dissatisfied	Neutral	Satisfied	Very Satisfied
☐	☐	☐	☐	☐

Interval Scale

Like nominal and ordinal scales, an interval scale measures the frequency at which the attribute is selected, and places attributes in order. The difference, however, is that interval data are continuous with equal distance between the response choices. What the interval scale lacks is a true zero.

The classic example of an interval scale is temperature. The difference in 90 degrees Fahrenheit and 80 degrees Fahrenheit is the same as the difference in 60 degrees Fahrenheit and 50 degrees Fahrenheit, which is 10 degrees. So the intervals between measures of temperature in Fahrenheit (degrees) are equal. However, when comparing temperatures, one cannot say that 100 degrees Fahrenheit is twice as hot as 50 degrees Fahrenheit. This is because temperature is measured on an interval scale. With interval scales, there is no true zero. This means that zero degrees Fahrenheit does not mean there is no temperature. Many states in the U.S. witness temperatures lower than zero degrees Fahrenheit each winter.

Test scores are an example of interval data. While the difference in a math test score of 40 and 50 is the same as the difference in a score of 70 and 80, it cannot be assumed that the person who scored 80 is twice as good at math as the person who scored a 40.

The classic linear, numeric rating scale is an interval-type scale. This scale asks the respondent to rate their attitude or perception along a numerical continuum, such as 1 to 5. This scale allows the surveyor to say that one score is higher or lower than another score at an equal distance. For example, if the scale is a rating on content usefulness at the end of a course, with 1 being not useful and 5 being useful, the researcher or evaluator could say that the rating of 5 (the highest rating of usefulness) is above the rating of 4 and that the distance between 5 and 4 is the same as between 4 and 3, which would be 1. They could also say that the difference between a score of 1 and 3 is the same as a score of 3 and 5, which would be 2. But, the researcher cannot say that course content is twice as useful to a person who scores "usefulness" a 4 as it is to one who scores "usefulness" a 2.

Because there is no true zero, arithmetic operations are limited to counting, ranking, and addition and subtraction. However, convention has led us to treat interval data the same as ratio data, using multiplication and division of responses to calculate a statistical mean for symmetrical data. An example of interval scales is shown in Table 7-3.

Table 7-3. Examples of Interval Scales

How important are the following topics to your success on the job?

	Extremely Unimportant				Extremely Important
	1	2	3	4	5
Survey objectives	☐	☐	☐	☐	☐
Question design	☐	☐	☐	☐	☐
Sampling	☐	☐	☐	☐	☐
Data analysis	☐	☐	☐	☐	☐
Reporting results	☐	☐	☐	☐	☐

In what year did you begin the program?

☐ 2007

☐ 2008

☐ 2009

☐ 2010

☐ 2011

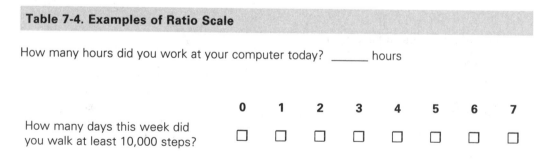

Noted

As previously mentioned, there is ongoing debate among researchers about whether to classify the Rensis Likert scale as ordinal or interval. The importance lies in the treatment of data during analysis (for example, the use of non-parametric versus parametric statistics). It is becoming common practice to assume Likert-type scales constitute interval-level measurement; however, some researchers contend that using parametric analysis for ordinal data is the first of "the seven deadly sins of statistical analysis." Others suggest while there is merit to the argument, sample size and distribution are more important than level of measurement in determining whether it is appropriate to use parametric statistics.

Ratio Scale

The fourth level of measurement in the Stevens framework is the ratio scale. Ratio scales have equal intervals and a true zero. The ratio scale is the highest level of measurement, in that all mathematical calculations apply. Ratios can be reported between any two given values on the scale. A ruler used to measure length in units of inches is a ratio scale because the ruler begins with a true zero. So, you can accurately state that a 6-inch plane is twice as long as a 3-inch plane. Examples of ratio measures are length, weight, money, time, and distance.

Because there is a true zero, we can count, rank, add and subtract, and multiply and divide the scale value. Table 7-4 shows examples of questions representing the ratio scale.

Table 7-4. Examples of Ratio Scale

How many hours did you work at your computer today? _____ hours

	0	1	2	3	4	5	6	7
How many days this week did you walk at least 10,000 steps?	☐	☐	☐	☐	☐	☐	☐	☐

Noted

Interval and ratio data are numeric and are considered quantitative. While technically they are different (one has a true zero, one has not), convention has led us to treat interval and ratio data the same, referring to these types of measurements as "numerical" rather than interval or ratio.

Descriptive Statistics

Statistics is the science of learning from data (Ott and Longnecker, 2010) that are categorized along the Stevens framework. Statistics help us understand those phenomena that we observe through implementation of survey projects. Through data analysis, we can describe a situation, compare relationships among measures, and predict outcomes. In relation to learning and development, performance improvement, HR, and meetings and events, statistics allows us to describe the perceptions, attitudes, knowledge, and behaviors of program participants. It allows us to predict outcomes and prescribe solutions.

Statistics provides us the tools to make sound judgment and decisions about issues. The accuracy or soundness of that judgment is dependent on:

- ▶ the number of data points in our analysis
- ▶ the sample size as compared to the population
- ▶ the statistics used given the type of data
- ▶ the type of data given the questions asked
- ▶ the uncertainty in our results—and there will always be some.

Descriptive statistics is the basis for all other statistics, and it is the first type of statistics you will run when you collect your data.

Noted

"Statistics means never having to say you're certain." —Derrick Niederman and David Boyum, *What the Numbers Say* (2003).

Descriptive statistics describes and summarizes quantitative data (or qualitative data that have been transformed into a numeric response using coded numbers). Descriptive statistics describes "what is" or "what the data say." It includes:

- ▶ Frequencies and proportions—how many and what percentage.
- ▶ Measures of central tendency—the central point of a group of data.
- ▶ Measures of dispersion—how spread out the data are.
- ▶ Coefficient of variation—the difference in variability between two measures.
- ▶ z-Score—how a single score relates to the mean.

Frequency and Proportions

The most basic form of data summary is the use of frequencies. It is the first type of analysis you should conduct for all of your survey projects. By reviewing the frequency distribution of your data, you can look for extreme data, missing data, and incorrect coding and data entries. For some survey questions in which response choices fall in either the nominal or ordinal categories, frequencies and proportions are the most appropriate statistics for reporting results as you use them to report the number of responses and the percentage of responses. Additionally, there are statistical tests, such as chi-square (described later), that can be applied to categorical data.

Frequency tables provide a simple display of data and are especially useful in describing categorical data. While the number of responses is often important, sometimes it is important to know the percentage of responses as well. For example, if someone says that 10 people reported that the training was no good, the next question that should be asked is: 10 of how many? On the other hand, if someone reports 50 percent of respondents provided evidence that they applied what they learned, the next question that should be asked is: 50 percent of how many? Table 7-5 shows a frequency table for a survey question. The first column includes the response choices and their respective coding values, along with a value for missing data. Column two is the frequency, which represents the number of people who responded and those who did not respond. A total of 19 surveys were entered into the system, but only 10 of the 19 people responded to this particular survey question.

Table 7-5. Frequency Table

Did your participation in the program have an influence in your remaining with the organization?

☐ Yes ☐ No ☐ Somewhat

		Frequency	Percent	Valid Percent	Cumulative Percent
Valid	0 **No**	7	36.8	70.0	70.0
	1 **Yes**	2	10.5	20.0	90.0
	2 **Somewhat**	1	5.3	10.0	100.0
	Total	10	52.6	100.0	
	9 **Missing**	9	47.4		
	Total	19	100.0		

Column three indicates the percentage of responses for each response choice, including the missing data. But, when we report results, we report not only the proportion of the total number of surveys, but more accurately the valid percent, which is the proportion of responses for those people who responded (column four). Column five describes the cumulative percent. As you can see, 70 percent of the people responded "No" and 90 percent responded either "No or Yes." All respondents either responded "No," "Yes," or "Somewhat."

Together, frequencies and proportions provide an adequate description of your data, particularly the initial view. But, you also need to be able to describe what is typical about the group you are surveying. That requires measures of central tendency.

Measures of Central Tendency

In summarizing distributions of values, the measure of central tendency is the most fundamental. This statistic also serves as the basis for most other statistical analysis, even the most complex inferential statistical procedures. Measures of central tendency describe what is "typical" of a group on a given measure. The definition of "typical" depends on the type of data and their distribution. There are three measures of central tendency:

▶ mode *(Mo)*
▶ median *(Mdn)*
▶ mean *(μ and $\bar{x}$).*

Different types of data use different measures of central tendency, as shown in Table 7-6.

Table 7-6. Measures of Central Tendency for Different Levels of Measurement

If the Data Are:	The Measure of Central Tendency Is:
Nominal	Mode
Ordinal	Median
	Mode
Interval/Ratio	Mean
	Median
	Mode

Think About This

Missing Data

Why is it important to account for missing data?

Suppose you implement a change initiative and you want to know how satisfied the management is with the implementation. You survey 100 managers and receive the following results:

Total number surveyed: 100

Respondents Satisfied: 55

Unsatisfied: 4

Missing: 41

What percentage of managers is satisfied with the change initiative?

If you report the percentage of managers satisfied as a proportion of the total number surveyed, you would report 55 percent. But if you report the percentage of managers who are satisfied as a proportion of those who respond, you would report 93 percent. This represents a different picture than the 55 percent.

So, whenever you face missing data, report both the percent and the valid percent, accounting for the missing data. This provides the most transparent picture possible.

The mode is the simplest summary of a variable and can be reported on categorical and numerical data. It is the only measure of central tendency for categorical data.

It indicates which category is the most common. In a frequency distribution, the mode is the value with the highest frequency or the response choice most often selected. To calculate the mode, the frequency with which values are assigned to a variable is counted; the value most frequently occurring is the mode. For example, suppose your survey question asks respondents to rank a list of tools most useful to them when they travel for work (see Table 7-2), and your responses come back as follows:

Dropbox
Dropbox
Evernote
Skype
Dropbox
iCloud
Skype
Dropbox
Evernote
Dropbox

The mode would be Dropbox. If your survey asks respondents to describe the importance of specific topics to their job success (see Table 7-3), the mode would be the most frequently selected response along the numerical scale.

The median is the score found in the middle of a series of values. To calculate the median, order the values in numerical order, then, locate the middle value. If there is an even number of values, the two middle values are totaled, and then halved.

The mean, also known as the arithmetic average, is the most often used measure of central tendency. The mean is used when working with interval/ratio data. While the mode and median can be used for numerical data, the mean is the preferred measure of central tendency, unless the distribution of values is skewed (such as in the case when measuring income for an entire customer base); in this case the preferred measure of central tendency is the median. Table 7-7 summarizes the levels of measurement and the measures of central tendency that describe the data categorized along those levels.

Table 7-7. Levels of Measurement

Levels of Measurement		Description	Sample Survey Question	Arithmetic Operations of Scale Values	Measure of Central Tendency
Categorical	Nominal	Responses with the same scale value or are the same on some attribute. The values of the scale have no "numeric" value.	What is your highest level of education? ☐ High School Graduate ☐ Four-Year Degree ☐ Master's Degree ☐ Doctoral Degree	Count	Mode
Categorical	Ordinal	Measures with a higher scale value have more of some attribute. The intervals between adjacent scale values lack mathematical meaning.	What type of training delivery do you prefer: ☐ Classroom ☐ Blended ☐ Online *** To what extent do you agree with the following: The course content is useful to my job? ☐ Strongly Disagree ☐ Disagree ☐ Neither Agree nor Disagree ☐ Agree ☐ Strongly Agree	Count Rank	Mode Median
Numerical	Interval	Intervals between adjacent scale values are equal with respect to the attribute being measured (e.g., the difference between 8 and 9 is the same as the difference between 76 and 77).	How satisfied were you with the training? Very Dissatisfied Very Satisfied 1 2 3 4 5 *** Please put a check mark in the space to show your opinion of how swiftly your luggage was transferred to baggage claim: Had to wait for luggage 1___ 2___ 3___ 4___ 5___ 6___ 7___ Luggage was waiting for me	Count Rank Add/Subtract *Multiply/Divide	Median for skewed data *Mean for symmetrical data
Numerical	Ratio	There is a rational zero point for the scale. Ratios are equivalent (e.g., the ratio of 2 to 1 is the same as the ratio of 8 to 4).	In how many training programs did you participate in 2011? _____	Count Rank Add/Subtract Multiply/Divide	Median for skewed data Mean for symmetrical data

*Convention has led us to treat interval the same as we treat ratio level data; hence interval and ratio data are often referred to as numerical.

Think About This

Calculate the Measure of Central Tendency

Using the data below, calculate the mean, median, and mode. The correct answer is found in Appendix A.

Measure of Central Tendency	Data	Answer
Mode	15, 20, 21, 20, 36, 15, 25, 15	
Median	15, 20, 21, 20, 36, 15, 25, 15	
Mean	15, 20, 21, 20, 36, 15, 25, 15	

Figure 7-1 shows three distributions of data and how the three types of measures of central tendency fit into the distribution. The first distribution shows a symmetrical distribution, also referred to as the "normal" distribution. In this distribution the mode, median, and mean are all the same. The second one shows a positively skewed distribution. Here, you see that the mode is to the far left, representing the most frequently selected values. The median is in the middle and the mean is to the far right. When data are skewed positively (or there is an extreme on the high side of the values), the mean will fall to the right of the median. On the other hand, the third distribution is negatively skewed indicating there are extreme data on the negative side.

While the mean is the arithmetic average, which offers greater utility than the other measures, it is also the measure of central tendency that is the most sensitive to extremes. This is why when we report income from a diverse group, we report the median rather than the mean. The mode should always be used for categorical data, as it reports the most frequently selected response.

Measures of Dispersion and Variation

When reporting results, it is important to report results in context. If you report that a set of survey responses has a mean of 20.88, the next question you need to answer is how much difference (spread) there is between the responses. Two distributions of data may have similar means yet very different values overall. In addition to measures of central tendency, analysts present measures of dispersion and variation that indicate the extent to which individual values in a distribution are different from each other.

Figure 7-1. Distributions

Symmetrical Distribution

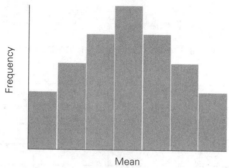

Positively Skewed Distribution

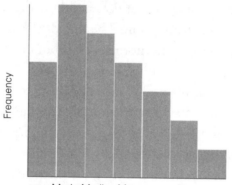

Negatively Skewed Distribution

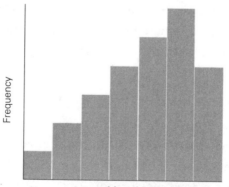

Measures of dispersion describe the uniformity of the data. Smaller values of dispersion for a variable imply more uniformity, whereas larger values imply more diversity. Some measures indicate only the difference between two observations in an ordered set of values. Other measures consider all observations in a distribution. Four common measures of dispersion and variation are:

- range
- interquartile range (IQR)
- variance (s^2 or σ^2)
- standard deviation (s or SD or σ).

The range is the simplest measure of dispersion. By simply subtracting the lowest score from the highest score, the range is developed. The range reports the difference between the largest and smallest measurements in a group and is the least useful of the measures of dispersion. Take a look at the example in Table 7-8. In the example there are two sets of test scores. The range in Test A is 40, whereas the range in Test B is 20. Hence, the variance in the scores for Test B is less because the difference between the high and the low scores is less.

Table 7-8. Calculating the Range

What is the range?

Test A		Test B	
50		65	
60	High = 90	68	High = 75
58	Low = 50	75	Low = 55
75	Range = 40	55	Range = 20
63		70	
90		69	
82		71	

Another measure of dispersion is the interquartile range (IQR). The IQR adjusts the range for the extreme values by calculating the difference between highest and lowest values of the 75th and the 25th percentiles rather than the entire frequency of numbers. To calculate, order the values and find the median. Then find the median of the upper and lower halves. Subtract the lower quartile from the upper quartile. Table 7-9 presents an example of the IQR.

Table 7-9. Calculating the Interquartile Range

What is the range?

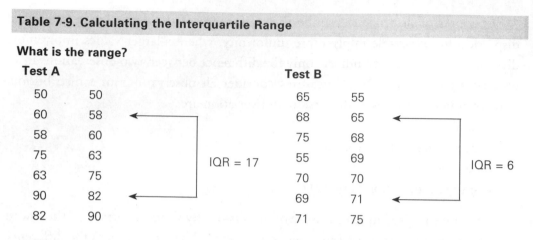

Test A			Test B		
50	50		65	55	
60	58		68	65	
58	60		75	68	
75	63	IQR = 17	55	69	IQR = 6
63	75		70	70	
90	82		69	71	
82	90		71	75	

The variance describes how close the values in a group of values are to the mean—the spread or dispersion of the values. The larger the variance, the more spread out the values are, affecting the reliability of the mean to be a predictor of what is typical in the population under study.

To calculate the variance of a sample set of data (denoted by s^2), you simply add the squared differences from the mean for all values (cases), then, divide the sum by the number of cases, minus one. Squaring the differences between the value and the mean makes the value positive and adds more weight to larger differences. Squaring also makes the mathematics manageable when using the variance in other calculations.

In formula form the equation is:

$$\text{Variance} = \frac{\text{Sum of squared distances from the mean for all cases}}{(\text{Number of cases} - 1)}$$

OR

$$s^2 = \frac{\Sigma(x_i - \bar{x})^2}{n - 1}$$

Noted

The use of n–1 in the denominator of the equation for the variance reduces the bias in the denominator, resulting in an estimate of the sample variance (s^2) that is closer to that of the population (σ^2).

The variance describes the dispersion of values around the mean using the square of the measurement units; however, because the differences are squared, the units are not the same as the actual units in the data. For example, if you were to report the variance in the distance walked in terms of steps, you would be reporting the squared steps. Or, if you were to report the variance in the size of groups participating in a program, you would be reporting squared groups of people. To provide a more accurate measure of variance—one that is in the same unit of measure as that which you are concerned—the standard deviation is the measure of choice.

The standard deviation (denoted by s) for a sample set of data is the square root of the variance. It converts the variance back to the specific unit of measure and identifies the variance in relation to the mean. In equation form the standard deviation is:

$$\text{Standard Deviation} = \sqrt{\frac{\text{Sum of squared distances from the mean for all cases}}{(\text{Number of cases} - 1)}}$$

OR

$$s = \sqrt{\frac{\Sigma(x_i - \bar{x})^2}{n - 1}}$$

Using our previous data on page 161 we calculate the range, variance, and standard deviation as follows:

- range = 21
- interquartile range = 9
- variance = 50.13
- standard deviation = 7.08

The standard deviation is appealing for a variety of reasons, but there are two specific reasons. One is that the standard deviation allows us to compare the difference of two or more sets of data. The second reason is that if the data set represents a normal distribution, we can use the Empirical Rule to interpret the standard deviation of a single set of measures.

The Empirical Rule is a statistical rule stating that, given a normal distribution of data, almost all data points should fall within three standard deviations of the mean. It allows us to draw conclusions about specific scores in the distribution. Table 7-10 presents the Empirical Rule.

Table 7-10. Empirical Rule

Given a normal distribution of data:

- Approximately 68% of the scores in the sample fall within one standard deviation of the mean.

- Approximately 95% of the scores in the sample fall within two standard deviations of the mean.

- Approximately 99% of the scores in the sample fall within three standard deviations of the mean.

For example, if the distribution was normal, and given the mean in our example is 20.88, and the standard deviation is 7.08, we can estimate that approximately 95 percent of the scores fall in the range of 20.88 -(2 x 7.08) to 20.88 +(2 x 7.08) or 6.72 to 35.04. This kind of information enables us to compare the performance of one variable with the performance of another, even when the variables are measured on entirely different scales.

Measures of central tendency and dispersion provide a first look at the survey data. They describe what typical responses look like and how different the variability within those responses is.

Think About This

Describe the Data

The table below is the output generated through Minitab, a statistical software package. The output describes the measures of central tendency and dispersion for the data from the above example. What can you say about the data?

N	Mean	StDev	Variance	Minimum	Median	Maximum	Range	Mode
8	20.88	7.08	50.13	15.00	20.00	36.00	21.00	15

Refer to Appendix A for our answer.

Coefficient of Variation

The coefficient of variation (CV) normalizes the standard deviation of two different measures so that comparisons in deviation can be made between those measures. It is a ratio of the standard deviation to the mean. In formula form it is:

$$CV = \frac{\text{Standard Deviation}}{\text{Mean}(\bar{x})} \times 100$$

Suppose you want to compare the variance in test scores with the variance in tenure with the organization of the people taking the tests. You could use the CV to normalize the standard deviation of both measures by dividing by the mean for the particular measure then multiplying by 100 to capture the percentage variation. For example, suppose the standard deviation for Test A is 13 and the mean score is 67. The CV would be 19 percent. The CV for tenure of people taking the test is 25 percent. Therefore, there is more variability in age than in test scores.

z-Score

One last statistic that may help you describe results is the standard score or z-score. The z-score expresses values in terms of units of the standard deviation. A z-score, for example, indicates that a specific case's value is 1.5 standard deviations above the mean. The z-score describes how many standard deviation units a single score is above or below the mean. It allows you to compare relative values of several different variables for one specific respondent.

To calculate the z-score:

$$\text{Standard score} = \frac{\text{Value} - \text{Mean}}{\text{Standard Deviation}}$$

OR

$$z = \frac{x_i - \bar{x}}{s}$$

Suppose as part of your health and wellness workshop, you provide content on the physiology of walking. You administer a survey that assesses participants' learning and provides them with a specific score that reflects their acquisition of the content knowledge. The average score for the group is 67 with a standard deviation of 13. One participant scores a 63 on her test. What is the z-score? What can you say about this individual score?

If you calculated a z-score of -0.31, you are correct. This tells you that the person's test score is 0.31 standard deviations below the average score. So, while a score of 63 appears much lower than a 67, when compared to the rest of the distribution, it is less than one standard deviation from the average.

Describing survey data is one step toward making meaning out of data, and in some instances, that is as far as you need to go. However, there are many times when you need to reach conclusions beyond a description of results. When that is the case, you will consider inferential statistics.

Inferential Statistics

While descriptive statistics allow us to describe our group, inferential statistics allow us to make generalizations, estimations, predictions, and decisions. For example, you might want to look at the difference between two groups, such as the difference between one group who receives training and the group that does not. Or you might want to know if there is a relationship between average test score and some measure of performance. Or maybe you want to provide evidence that the Western region is more fit than the Eastern region as a result of participation in the wellness program. These issues can be addressed by looking at the relationship between measures and the significance of those relationships through inferential statistics. A variety of types of statistical tests are available to us. Some of the most commonly used include:

- ▶ Chi-square: the extent to which observed frequencies differ from expected frequencies.
- ▶ T-test: compares the differences in the means of two measures.
- ▶ Analysis of variance: analyzes the effect of categorical variables on a continuous outcome variable.
- ▶ Linear regression: the extent to which performance in one measure predicts that in another.
- ▶ Structural equation modeling: advanced statistical technique that allows researchers to diagram relationships between multiple independent and dependent variables.

Chi-Square

The chi-square (X^2) test is a popular statistical test because it is easy to calculate and interpret. The purpose of the chi-square test is to determine whether observed frequencies differ significantly from the frequencies expected. This test is used to compare two nominal variables, ordinal variables (scaled responses), or a combination of nominal and ordinal. The chi-square test measures the significance of cross-tabulations. Chi-square values should not be calculated for percentages. The cross-tabs must be converted into absolute values (numbers) before performing the test. It is problematic when any cell is less than five.

T-Test

The t-test helps us infer the differences between the means of two measures for one group or the differences in means for one measure between groups. While chi-square is used with two nominal variables, ordinal variables, or a combination, the t-test applies to interval and ratio data. It is probably the most commonly used statistical test in learning and development, as it is often used when evaluating programs and comparing differences in performance between groups that attend programs and groups that do not.

There are three specific types of t-tests. One is the *one-sample t* where the mean of a measure for a group is compared to a norm or standard value. For example:

Students of cohort 1 in the RSU master's program receive an average of 85 on the midterm. How does this compare to the average of the midterm average for the other 10 cohorts who participated in the program?

In this example, the mean of the group is compared to a norm (the average score of the other 10 cohorts).

The formula for the one-sample t-test, is as follows:

$$t = \frac{\bar{x} - \mu}{s / \sqrt{n}}$$

where

$\bar{x}$ = sample mean (post-program measurement or experimental group measurement)
μ = population mean (preprogram measurement or control group measurement)
s = sample standard deviation
n = sample size (number of participants).

A second type of t-test is the *dependent t*. Here, the mean of a measure for a group is compared to the mean of a measure for the same group at a different time period. An example follows.

Do average scores on the health inventory change for 50 men at the local frozen food plant after they participate in a low-fat diet program?

In this case, the heath inventory is taken two times. The t-test is run to determine if there is a significant difference in the mean for each test score average.

The third type of t-test is the *independent t*. This t-test compares the mean of a measure for two independent groups. Here is an example.

Is the average increase in sales for the program group significantly higher than the average increase in sales for the control group?

In this case, there are two independent groups. One group participates in a program, the other does not. After the program, the average sales for the two groups are compared and evaluated using the independent t-test.

Analysis of Variance

Analysis of Variance (ANOVA) is a statistical technique for assessing the difference between data sets. It assesses how nominal independent variables influence a continuous dependent variable. It assumes that the populations for all groups being compared have equal standard deviations (assumption of homogeneity of variance), and that the samples are randomly selected from the population. The tests in ANOVA are based on the *F*-ratio, the variation due to an experimental treatment or effect divided by the variation due to experimental error.

The good news for all of these statistical procedures is that they are so basic that most survey software packages can develop them for you. If not with your survey software, then use Excel, Minitab, SPSS, SAS, or some other program. The key is to recognize what they are and how to use them; then, let your software do the work.

Correlation Analysis

Occasionally you may want to describe how two measures relate to each other. If this is the case, you would compute the correlation coefficient. This statistic describes the amount of variability shared between two measures and what they have in common. It is a measure of association. An example of use might be if you want to know if there is a relationship between participant test scores resulting from a program (x) and how their level of production is on the job (y).

There are several correlation coefficients. The type of correlation procedure you use depends on the type of data in terms of level of measurement (nominal, ordinal, interval or ratio). One commonly used is the Pearson product-moment correlation coefficient, which applies to interval data. The equation for a simple Pearson product-moment correlation is:

$$r = \frac{n\Sigma x_i y_i - (\Sigma x_i)(\Sigma y_i)}{\sqrt{\{n(\Sigma x_i^2)-(\Sigma x_i)^2\}\{n\Sigma y_i^2-(\Sigma y_i)^2\}}}$$

where

r_{xy} is the correlation coefficient between x and y

n is the sample size

x_i is the individual's score on the x variable

y_i is the individual's score on the y variable

$x_i y_i$ is the product of each x score times its corresponding y score

x^2 is the individual x score, squared

y^2 is the individual y score, squared

The results of the analysis may look something like the data in table 7-11 below:

Table 7-11. Data for Calculating Correlation Coefficient

Item Number	Program Test Score	Production Efficiency	x_i^2	y_i^2	$x_i y_i$
1	75	105	5625*	11025†	7875‡
2	68	95	4624	9025	6460
3	88	116	7744	13456	10208
4	92	119	8464	14161	10948
5	78	111	6084	12321	8658
6	82	113	6724	12769	9266
7	74	100	5476	10000	7400
8	90	120	8100	14400	10800
9	95	125	9025	15625	11875
Total	742	1004	61866	112782	83490

Sample calculations:

* $x_i^2 = 75 \times 75 = 5625$ † $y_i^2 = 105 \times 105 = 11025$ ‡ $x_i y_i = 75 \times 105 = 7875$

By inputting the numbers into the equation above, the results are:

$$r = \frac{9(83490)-(742)(1004)}{\sqrt{\{9(61866)-(742)^2\}\{9(112782)-(1004)^2\}}} = \frac{6442}{\sqrt{(6230)(7022}} = .97$$

So what does r = .97 mean? The value of the correlation coefficient ranges between a perfect negative correlation score of -1.0; a perfect positive correlation of 1.0. Everything else in between describes some degree of positive or negative correlation. Table 7-12 provides a continuum of the strength and direction of correlations based on the correlation coefficient. Note that the absolute value correlation coefficient denotes the strength of the relationship. For example a -.80 is stronger than a .60.

Table 7-12. Interpretation of Correlation Coefficient

	Interpretations
Correlation Value	General Description
-1.0	Perfect negative correlation
-.8 to -1.0	Very high degree of negative correlation
-.6 to -.8	High degree of negative correlation
-.4 to -.6	Medium degree of negative correlation
-.2 to -.4	Low degree of negative correlation
+.2 to -.2	Probably no correlation
+.2 to +.4	Low degree of positive correlation
+.4 to +.6	Medium degree of positive correlation
+.6 to +.8	High degree of positive correlation
+.8 to +1.0	Very high degree of positive correlation
+1.0	Perfect positive correlation

Linear Regression

Building on the correlation coefficient is linear regression. Linear regression allows us to make predictions about future outcomes of measure using a set of previously collected data. For example, let's say you know there is a correlation between participant test scores (x) and production (y). You want to use this relationship to predict production based on the test scores from another group of participants. To do this you will create a regression equation and use that to plot a regression line that looks similar to that shown in Figure 7-2. The regression line is the best guess what production will be based on a test score. The distance between each data point and the regression line is the error in that prediction—it is a direct reflection of the correlation between the two variables (see Figure 7-2).

Figure 7-2. Regression Line

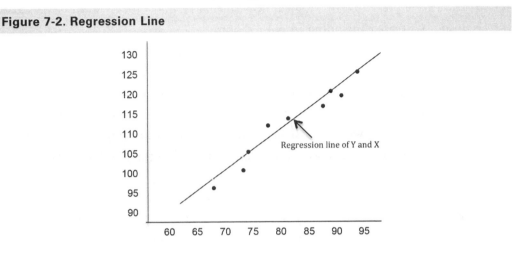

Structural Equation Modeling

Structural equation modeling, or SEM, is a sophisticated statistical procedure that allows you to build a structure of the relationships between multiple independent and dependent variables. It allows you to diagram a path between those relationships. Structural equation modeling can be used to determine the key factors of importance so that decision makers can focus on those factors. By using SEM, you can identify the most critical measures to take for a given situation, and focus your survey instrument on those specific measures. This not only reduces the number of survey items, but helps ensure that you collect the most meaningful data. For example, KnowledgeAdvisors used SEM to develop the critical path from participant reaction to a program and job performance (KnowledgeAdvisors, 2009).

Reporting Results

Reporting results is the icing on the cake. You've designed a good survey, had successful response, and have conducted the appropriate analysis. All that is left is to package the results in such a way that stakeholders value the information.

There are two fundamental issues when it comes to report development: 1) the report outline and narrative and 2) the graphical display of data.

Report Outline and Narrative

When developing the report outline for your survey project, keep in mind that you are writing for the audience, not you. Words need to be crisp and clean and the content should be presented in a logical flow so that readers quickly know where the story is going. Consider including in your report:

▶ Abstract of about 150 to 250 words that quickly gets to the crux of your report.

▶ Executive summary, providing enough detail so readers accept the results as credible and can quickly identify next steps and what's in it for them.

▶ Table of contents with at least first and second-level headings.

▶ List of tables and figures so readers can quickly find the graphic displays of data.

▶ Glossary of terms so readers don't get lost in terminology.

▶ Statement of need and survey objectives to set the stage for results.

▶ Methodology to bring credibility to your findings and to ensure readers can easily put the results into some context.

▶ Results beginning with a description of respondents and working through to the highlights.

▶ Conclusions drawn from the findings.

▶ Recommendations tied to the findings and conclusions, along with specific next steps and a timeline if appropriate.

▶ References to show you have done your homework.

▶ Appendix that includes the survey instrument and all related correspondence, raw data, and verbatim comments that have been summarized in the findings section.

If you are reading this book while working on your graduate thesis or doctoral dissertation, be sure to refer to your graduate program for the specific outline they expect you to follow. Most research books offer outlines for quantitative and qualitative studies. Your organization or institution of higher learning may have its own outline, so begin there so you can plan accordingly.

Use crisp, direct sentences. This approach is much more powerful than long, drawn out sentences that take longer to read than the value of the sentence. Get to the point without missing important information. Refer to tables and graphics by name or by number rather than by saying "the table below," and refer to them in the text prior to inserting the table. Readers will get lost and start looking for the table. Be as specific as possible.

Basic Rule

Describe tables and figures in the narrative immediately before inserting the table. Insert tables or figures after the description.

The text of the report describes the findings, but must also interpret the findings for the reader. As you write up the findings, ask yourself, "So what?" to make sure what you are reporting is providing useful information. When you make a claim about a finding, be sure to back it up.

Plan on multiple revisions to your report. Many writing textbooks suggest that writers "write for the trash can" the first time out. Just get the words down; then edit the document with a critical eye. If possible, have someone with less familiarity with the project take a pass at it. Sometimes, when you own the project, you are too close to it and miss items that may be important to your audience. Allreck and Settle (1995) provide a good set of guidelines for developing the narrative for your report. These guidelines are shown in Table 7-13.

Table 7-13. Guidelines for Developing Narrative for Final Report

1. Divide the text into major sections according to the types of information needs, topics, or issues.
2. Include the tables after they have been referenced in the text, not before.
3. Avoid technical jargon used in statistics or processing in favor of simpler, layperson's vocabulary.
4. Use short, simple, direct sentences rather than long, complex ones.
5. Use nouns repetitively to avoid any confusion about the antecedent of pronouns such as it, them, they, and so on.
6. In references to tables, figures, and other inclusions, identify them by their number or letter rather than by indefinite terms such as "the table."
7. Make the text interpretive rather than just descriptive of the results.
8. Introduce each major section by identifying its purpose or the reason for including it.
9. Discuss the major facts or relationships contained in each table or figure, but make the text fairly independent so it's meaningful without reference to tables.
10. Include additional ideas, conclusions, or suggestions, based on previous experience or intuition, but clearly note when they go beyond the actual results.

Source: Alreck, P.L. and Settle, R.B. (1995). *The Survey Research Handbook: Guidelines and Strategies for Conducting a Survey,* 2nd edition. New York: McGraw-Hill.

Table 7-14. Report Outline

Measuring the ROI in Meetings and Events

The report outline should have a logical flow. Readers should be able to quickly see the key components of the report. Table 7-14 is an outline of an ROI impact study that relied heavily on survey data.

Graphical Displays of Data

Some say a picture paints a thousand words. The question is: Are the pictures painting the right words on the canvas? Tufte (1997, 1983), Few (2009, 2004), and Harris (1999), along with others, have written volumes about how to best display quantitative and qualitative data. Information graphics and data visualization are the hot topics of the day, and it is no wonder. With the increasing emphasis on measurement, evaluation, ROI, and complex analytics, we need to be able to report data in compelling ways that inspire action.

In this section, we are covering only the basics of graphical displays of data. But it is sometimes the basics that we forget and we end up misrepresenting findings. The basics include pie charts, bar charts and histograms, line graphs, and tabular displays.

Pie Charts

Some of our data visualization experts scoff at pie charts. However, they are still standard graphs when you want to compare a part to the whole. Pie charts are used to display the percentage of a total number of measures falling within different categories. According to Harris (1999), one advantage of using pie charts is that people naturally think of a circle as encompassing 100 percent of whatever is being depicted. Figure 7-3 demonstrates a pie chart showing the percentage of sales representatives for each division the organization serves. This simple chart tells sales managers in what regions sales representatives are located.

Figure 7-3. Pie Chart

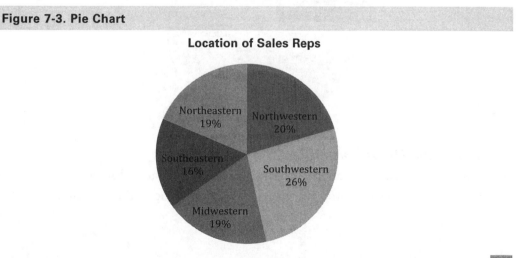

To improve the visibility of the data in a pie chart, place the data in some order, reorder the data so there is a clockwise progression, and then shade the slices so that the order is evident. While the figure is still "just a pie chart," data order and shading can provide a clearer message. If you want to highlight the southwestern division, pull out the slice. These displays are shown in Figure 7-4.

Figure 7-4. Alternative Displays Using Pie Charts

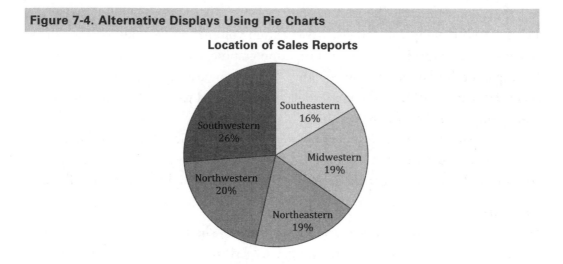

Location of Sales Reports

Remove a slice to highlight one region.

Location of Sales Reps

Bar Charts and Histograms

Bar charts are another type of chart that does not excite many. But they are so useful that it is hard to get away from them. Bar charts are not to be confused with histograms.

Histograms, like those in Figure 7-1, represent continuous, numerical data. Bar charts are displays of categorical data. Each bar is constructed at the category of the measure, and the height of the bar is equal to the frequency (count) of each category. Figure 7-5 demonstrates a simple bar chart using our sales representative data.

Figure 7-5. Bar Chart

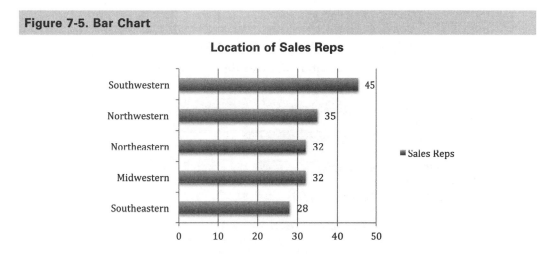

With bar charts we can combine variables and make comparisons of our descriptive data. Figure 7-6 shows a bar chart comparing the number of sales representatives in each region for 2011 and 2012. This simple picture shows a change in the distribution of sales representatives among regions.

Figure 7-6. Bar Chart Comparing 2011 and 2012 Sales Reps

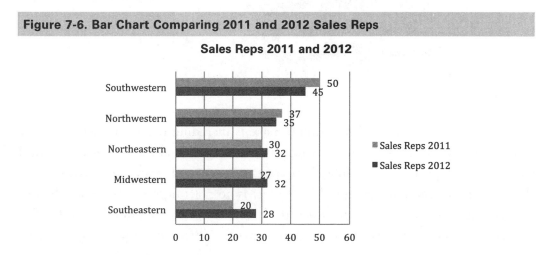

We often make the mistake of trying to improve upon our displays by putting them in a three-dimensional form. Software packages allow us many opportunities to dress up our data displays. But, as our parents told us as we were growing up: "Just because you can, doesn't mean you should." Figure 7-7 compares a standard bar chart to a three-dimensional version. Look at them from the perspective of visibility of data rather than the perspective of what looks more interesting. Does the standard bar more clearly focus on the data?

Figure 7-7. Basic Bar Chart Compared to 3-D Bar Chart

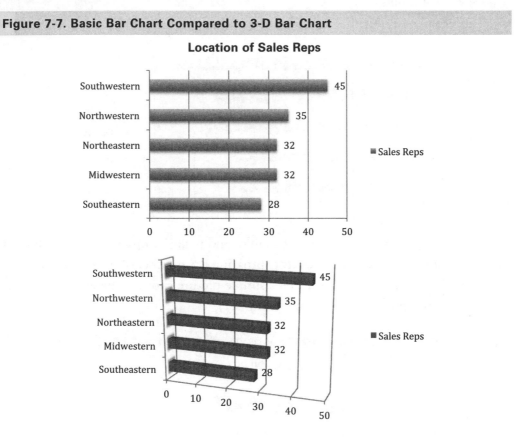

Another mistake we will sometimes make is including too many tick marks or too few tick marks to make the data display meaningful. Take a look at the vertical bar charts in Figure 7-8. The first chart appears to have too many tick marks, while the second does not have enough. While there is no exact number that works best in all circumstances, the longer the scale, the more tick marks it should include. The third chart appears to have just enough to show the difference in the range of sales.

Figure 7-8. Bar Charts: Too Many vs. Too Few Tick Marks

Monthly Sales

Too Many Too Few About Right

Line Graphs

Line graphs are useful displays, particularly if you are tracking data over time. Data displayed using line graphs is numerical rather than categorical. Figure 7-9 presents a simple line graph showing monthly sales for two products. Line charts are useful for finding trends in data. Many of the data you are collecting may be best displayed using a line chart.

Figure 7-9. Line Charts

There are many ways in which you can display data. The techniques just described are the most common and are the basis for some of the more complex displays.

Tabular Displays of Data

There are many, many ways you can display data. As previously mentioned, interest in information graphics and visualization of data is growing. So the more you know, the more prepared you will be when your survey data are ready for summarizing. But probably the most flexible—and often the best—communication channel for data, particularly descriptive data, are tables. Creating tables is not too difficult, given that survey technology almost does it for you.

There are two decisions you as the researcher need to make when creating tables. The first is the format and the second is labeling. Format requires simple rows and columns, with enough white space so that the tables and data do not appear too cluttered. Also, to the extent possible, keep your pages vertical (portrait). While there are some tables that require pages to be laid out in landscape, try to make reading tables easy on the reader and format them for vertical display. Also, use a standard format when possible so the reader can quickly recognize the type of data being presented.

Labels should be clear and consistent. They should reflect the data you are presenting and help the table speak for itself rather than clutter the table. Rows and columns should both be labeled.

One tabular display that you may be interested in is one that displays Likert-scale data. As we mentioned multiple times, the Likert scale is technically an ordinal scale in which the data are categorical in nature, and respondents are marking the scale in terms of their preferences. This makes the data ordinal. All too often, people will report Likert scale data as if it is numerical. But in reality, the data are categorical and are such that the results should be presented as proportions of the number of people who responded. Table 7-15 shows an example of a display of Likert-scale data. Given that the data are categorical, the percentage of frequency with which each response was chosen is the most appropriate statistic. You would not want to capture the mean, because the data are not numerical. Even if you presented the data with numerical codes 1 to 15, the data would technically not be numerical. Simple tables such as this can be a powerful display of data.

Basic Rule
Design tables so that they speak for themselves.

Table 7-15. Likert Scale Results

How much do you agree or disagree with each statement?

	Strongly Agree	Agree	Neutral	Disagree	Strongly Disagree
Walking is good for overall health and well-being.	8.4%	11.5%	27.7%	36.5%	15.9%
10,000 steps a day is a reasonable number of steps, given my schedule.	12.9%	16.2%	19.1%	31.5%	20.3%
Employees should be allowed to walk outside during lunch.	6.5%	19.4%	24.9%	29.5%	19.6%
Employees should be allowed to walk 30 minutes outside anytime of the day.	10.4%	18.0%	16.5%	26.2%	28.9%
Pedometers are good tools for tracking how far I walk.	16.%	18.3%	19.0%	22.1%	24.0%
Tracking my daily walks in the health and wellness journal will help me achieve results.	21.5%	26.4%	18.2%	13.5%	20.4%

N=325

Infographics

The growing interest in analytics and the need to communicate complex data and information in such a way that resonates with all audiences has placed new emphasis on information graphics, or infographics. Infographics are a combination of statistical output and qualitative storytelling in one graphic. Charles Minard's 1869 chart showing the number of men in Napoleon's 1812 Russian campaign army, their movement, and the temperature changes they experienced along the way is one of the most noted information graphics by experts in visualization of data. The graph shows how the army began with 422,000 troops and ended with only 10,000 troops. This chart is shown in Figure 7-10.

The fundamental principle of infographics is to display complex information in a clear, convenient, and compelling way so that the audience gets the message fast. According to ilimitado 3D Graphics, the basic principles of infographics are that an infographic:

  ▸ must be global and universal in format
  ▸ shows and reveals information which was previously hidden, taboo, unclear, or even unrevealed

▶ describes visually things that contribute to understanding its content easier, such as a figure or something related to the information

▶ is a visual view with words and image

▶ is stand-alone and must have clear information so there is no question raised when people see it

▶ must give readers the right understanding about the information.

Figure 7-10. Infographic: Minard's Chart Showing Napoleon's March on Russia

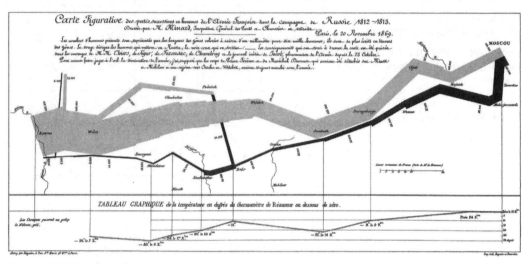

Source: By Charles Minard (1781-1870) via Wikimedia Commons

*This work is in the **public domain** in the United States, and those countries with a copyright term of life of the author plus **100** years or less. This file has been identified as being free of known restrictions under copyright law, including all related and neighboring rights.*

While infographics provide an interesting view of data, it is possible that the graphic distorts the information. Ensuring that differences in data are of an appropriate scale will provide viewers a more accurate view of the information. Also, while developing infographics can be fun and entertaining, too much of a good thing can reap an opposite effect than planned. So, ensure that every bit of information on the infographic is useable information.

Data summary and reporting is the end result of good survey design—but it is the end that matters most. Inappropriate data analysis for the questions you ask on a survey can hurt your credibility. Ineffective reporting can result in misinterpretation of information and poor decision making.

Getting It Done

It is time for you to summarize your data and start putting together that final report. Using the ASTD Measurement/ROI blog and resources at the ROI Institute, we will continue the conversation about data analysis, data summary, and reporting.

8

Sample Surveys

· ·

What's Inside This Chapter

This chapter gives examples of actual surveys used for collecting data for the following. Upon completion of this chapter, you will have reviewed the following surveys.

▶ End-of-course questionnaire for an automotive company
▶ Structured interview survey for a gap analysis of a software company's learning and development function
▶ Follow-up survey for a caseworker development program for an Australian government agency
▶ Follow-up interview questions for succession planning program
▶ Employee survey for a U.S. Department of Defense agency
▶ Follow-up questionnaire for a leadership development program
▶ A culture of innovation leadership survey

Sample Surveys

If you have read the book in its entirety, you now know the basics of survey design. Even though the example survey questions throughout the book may have been helpful, it sometimes helps even more to see an actual example of a full survey. So, in this chapter, we are providing seven different surveys. We hope they will prove to be helpful as you decide what questions to ask and how to ask them for your next survey project. Please note that the surveys are examples intended to help you generate ideas. Please request permission from the contributors before you replicate their work.

End-of-Course Evaluation
Multinational Automotive Company

Purpose
The purpose of this survey was to describe participant reaction to the sales training program at a multi-national automotive company.

Objectives
The following objectives serve as the basis for this survey:

1. Determine participant perception of knowledge/skills acquired.
2. Determine participant perception of instructor effectiveness.
3. Determine participant perception of content.
4. Identify opportunites for course improvement.

Source
Weber, E. (2013). Solution Selling for Sales Reps. In *Measuring the Success of Sales Training: A Step-by-Step Guide to Measuring Impact and Calculating ROI*, eds. P.P. Phillips, J.J. Phillips, and R. Robinson. Alexandria, VA: ASTD Press.

Table 8-1. End-of-Course Evaluation

Name:	Course Title: MAC Sales Training
Dealership:	Instructor:
Position:	Date:

We would appreciate your evaluation of this course. Please tick the relevant rating boxes.

Objectives: As a result of this training course I am able to:	Strongly Disagree	Mostly Disagree	Neither Agree nor Disagree	Mostly Agree	Strongly Agree
	1	2	3	4	5
Make a clear distinction between premium selling and other forms of selling.					
Describe the expectations of a customer buying a MAC brand.					
Explain the skills required by a successful sales consultant.					
Give and receive feedback and use feedback for self-development.					
Explain to others my personal strengths and development areas.					
Show how to make a good first impression and its importance in sales.					
Demonstrate the range of questions and techniques that can be used in sales.					
Explain the difference between emotional and rational focus of the customer.					
Practice active listening.					
Use positive body language and other nonverbal signals.					
Deliver a variety of closing techniques.					
Instructor Evaluation	**1**	**2**	**3**	**4**	**5**
The instructors demonstrated a thorough knowledge of the subject(s).					
The instructors' explanations were easy to understand.					
Course Evaluation	**1**	**2**	**3**	**4**	**5**
The course content was relevant to my role in the dealership.					
The course materials were easy to understand.					
The course provided me with adequate opportunity for involvement.					
What changes, if any, should we make to this training course?					
What did you find to be of the most value in this training course?					
General comments:					
Action Plan: When you return to the dealership, what initial steps will you take to apply your knowledge/skills?					

GAP Analysis Structured Interview
Software Company

Purpose
The purpose of this survey was to determine gaps in performance of the learning and development function.

Objectives
The following program objectives served as the basis for the survey objectives:

1. Determine the alignment between learning and development activities and business needs.
2. Determine the frequency with which, when conducting a needs assessment, learning and development professionals identify payoff needs, business needs, performance needs, learning needs, and preference needs.
3. Determine the frequency with which the learning and development function evaluates programs to each of the five levels of evaluation.
4. Identify criteria used for implementing learning programs.
5. Determine current approach to evaluating learning and development programs as compared to stakeholders' expectations.

Source
Phillips, J.J. (2012). ROI Institute, Inc.

Table 8-2. Gap Analysis Structured Interview

GAP Analysis Questionnaire

For Needs Assessment, Business Alignment, and Evaluation

for Sales Training Programs at a Software Company

Instructions: Please provide your responses to the following questions/issues and include supporting information on each of the items.

Part I. Initial Analysis: Beginning With the End in Mind

1. What is your definition of value as it relates to sales training and enablement? Check all that apply.
    Value must:

    ___Be balanced, with qualitative and quantitative data

    ___Contain financial and non-financial perspectives

    ___Reflect strategic and tactical issues

    ___Satisfy all key stakeholders

    ___Be consistent in collection and analysis

    ___Be grounded in conservative standards

    ___Come from credible sources

What would you add to the list?

_____

_____

_____

2. Recently, have you had more requests to show business impact, monetary value, or the financial ROI from programs? ☐Yes ☐ No
    If yes, which of the following do you think is driving the request?

    ___Top executive requirement

    ___The total cost of a program

    ___Increased pressures for improved efficiency

    ___Competitive pressures for funding

    ___Lack of success in previous efforts to show value

    ___Client requires it

Can you provide your internal correspondence on this issue? ☐Yes ☐No

3. As programs are delivered, to what extent have you taken a results-based approach compared to activity-based? The following eight items list the elements associated with each approach. Please indicate the extent to which you have focused on a results-based approach, using a rating scale of 1-5. ("1" is the activity-based approach; "5" is the results-based.) Place a number under the rating column for each of the items.

Activity vs. Results					
Activity-Based				**Results-Based**	Rating
1	**2**	**3**	**4**	**5**	
1 No business need for the program.			Program linked to specific business needs.		
2 No assessment of performance issues.			Assessment of performance effectiveness.		
3 No specific measurable objectives beyond learning.			Specific objectives for application and business impact.		
4 No effort to prepare program participants to achieve results.			Results expectations communicated to participants.		
5 No effort to prepare the work environment to support transfer.			Environment prepared to support transfer.		
6 No efforts to build partnerships with key managers.			Partnerships established with key managers and clients.		
7 No measurement of results or benefit-cost analysis.			Measurement of results and benefit-cost analysis.		
8 Planning and reporting is input-focused.			Planning and reporting is outcome-focused.		

Can you provide documentation on your results-based process? ☐Yes ☐No

4. What are the reasons for sales training and enablement programs? Please indicate the percent of programs initiated for the reasons listed below. A rough estimate is OK; the total should be 100 percent.

The Reasons for Training Programs

The program is a result of:

- A needs analysis that was conducted _____
- A management request _____
- Other organizations in industry are implementing it _____
- A trend _____
- The team suggesting that it was needed _____
- A need to support new systems, processes, or technology _____

- A need to support other programs such as continuous process improvement _____
- Other _____

Total 100%

Can you provide your guidelines on these issues? ☐Yes ☐No

5. Refer to the V-model, which connects the needs assessment with evaluation. On the left side of the V-model are the five levels of needs assessment and analysis. Please respond to the series of questions on the next page.

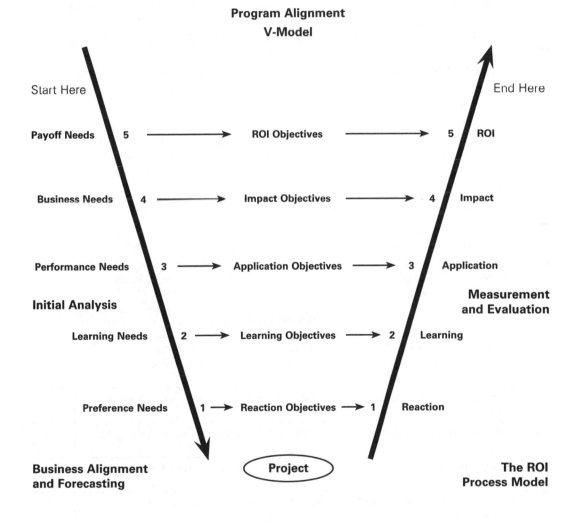

Program Alignment
V-Model

Initial Analysis and Assessment

Here are the definitions:

5) **Payoff needs** address the issue of the importance of the proposed request for training or enablement. This level addresses the question: Is this a problem worth solving or an opportunity worth pursuing? _____%

4) **Business needs** connect the project to specific business measures usually defined as an output, quality, cost, or time. For the sales area, the project should connect to sales, market share, new accounts, customer loyalty, customer retention, etc. _____%

3) **Performance needs** identifies specific performances of individuals that are influencing the particular business need. Essentially this level addresses the question: What are the target participants doing or not doing that's influencing the business measure?_____%

2) **Learning needs** describe what specifically the target participants need to know or do to achieve the performance in question. _____%

1) **Preference needs** defines the desired preferences for a particular project or program. For the participants, the preferences define the reaction desired from the participants. _____%

For each of the above, indicate what percent of programs are assessed at that level. For example, if every program has a learning needs assessment, the response would be 100 percent. If only 10 percent of the programs are analyzed at business need level, then 10 percent would be entered.

Can you provide examples of Level 5, 4, and 3 analyses above?   ☐Yes   ☐No

Part II. Program Objectives

6.   Please indicate the extent to which your programs have these specific objectives. Indicate the percent of programs that currently have these objectives in place.

Objectives	
1. **Reaction objectives** define specifically how participants should react to the program (e.g., relevant to their work, important to their own success, intent to use, etc.).	
2. **Learning objectives** define specific skills and knowledge needed that will be learned in the program.	
3. **Application objectives** define specifically how participants should apply what they've learned.	
4. **Impact objectives** define the specific business measure or measures that will be influenced by the program.	
5. **ROI objectives** define the minimum acceptable return on investment in the project.	

Can you provide examples of application and impact objectives?   ☐Yes   ☐No

Part III. Measurement and Evaluation

7. Indicate that the current percent of programs that are evaluated at each of the levels below, and indicate your goal for evaluating at each level. The best practice recommendations are provided and our most recent benchmarking is included.

	Measurement in the Learning and Development Field				
Level	Measurement Category	Current Status*	Best Practice*	Your Goal*	Comments About Status*
0	**Inputs/Indicators** Measures inputs into learning and development including the number of programs, participants, costs, and efficiencies	100%	100%		This is being accomplished now 100% †
1	**Reaction and Planned Action** Measures reaction to, and satisfaction with, the experience, contents, and value of program		100%		Need more focus on content and perceived value 79% †
2	**Learning** Measures what participants learned in the program—information, knowledge, skills, and contacts (take-aways from the program)		80–90%		Must use simple learning measures 54% †
3	**Application** Measures progress after the program—the use of information, knowledge, skills, and contacts		30%		Need more follow-up 31% †
4	**Business Impact** Measures changes in business impact variables such as output, quality, time, and cost—linked to the program		10%		This is the connection to business impact 14.4% †
5	**ROI** Compares the monetary benefits of the business impact measures to the costs of the program.		5%		The ultimate level of evaluation 4.3% †

* Percent of programs evaluated at this level

† Best practice benchmarking (ROI Methodology user for five-plus years)

» **Add your numbers in each box for current status and your goal.**

Can you provide documentation on your approach to these issues?   ☐Yes   ☐No

8. Please indicate the current criteria used for selecting programs for Level 4 and 5
    evaluations. Please check all that apply.

Criteria for Selecting Programs for Level 4 and Level 5 Evaluations
___Life cycle of the program
___Linkage of program to operational goals and issues
___Importance of program to strategic objectives
___Executive interest in the evaluation
___Cost of the program
___Visibility of the program
___Size of target audience
___Investment of time required

Can you provide guidelines for this issue? ☐Yes ☐No

9. Below are the typical data collection methods used to collect data for the first four levels
    of evaluation. The check mark indicates that the instrument is typically used for that level
    of evaluation. Please indicate your top three instruments for Level 3 and Level 4 by
    indicating a number 1 for most used, 2 for second most, and 3 is third most used.

Data Collection During and After Program					
Method	Level	1	2	3	4
• Surveys		✓	✓	✓	
• Questionnaires		✓	✓	✓	✓
• Observation			✓	✓	
• Interviews				✓	
• Focus Groups				✓	
• Tests/Quizzes			✓		
• Demonstrations			✓		
• Simulations			✓		
• Action planning/Improvement plans				✓	✓
• Performance contracting				✓	✓
• Performance monitoring					✓

Can you provide your guidelines for data collection? ☐Yes ☐No

10. When a program is evaluated at the impact level, the effects of the program must be isolated from other influences. Which specific techniques are you using to isolate the effects of your programs on the data? Check all that apply.

Methods to Isolate Program Effects

___Use of a control group arrangement

___Trend-line analysis of performance data

___Use of forecasting methods of performance data

___Participant's estimate of program impact (percent)

___Supervisor's estimate of program impact (percent)

___Manager's estimate of program impact

___Use of expert/previous studies

___Calculate/estimate the impact of other factors

___Customer input

Can you provide guidelines on this issue? ☐Yes ☐No

11. When calculating ROI, business data must be converted to money. Sometimes the money is available as a standard value, and other times, experts and databases can be used. Which of the following methods are used to convert data to money?

Methods to Convert Data to Money

___Converting output to contribution—standard value

___Converting the cost of quality—standard value

___Converting employee's time—standard value

___Using historical costs

___Using internal and external experts

___Using data from external databases

___Linking with other measures

___Using participants' estimates

___Using supervisors' and managers' estimates

___Using staff estimates

Can you provide guidelines on this issue? ☐Yes ☐No

12. Below are the costs that are often included in an ROI analysis. When ROI analyses have been conducted, to what extent have all of these cost categories been included? Mark an X by any that are <u>not</u> included in the ROI analysis.

Fully Loaded Cost Categories		
<u>Cost Item</u>	**<u>Prorated</u>**	**<u>Expensed</u>**
Needs Assessment	✓	
Design and Development	✓	
Acquisition/Purchase (if applicable)	✓	
Delivery/Implementation		✓
• Salaries/Benefits—Facilitator Time		✓
• Salaries/Benefits—Coordination Time		✓
• Program Materials and Fees		✓
• Travel/Lodging/Meals		✓
• Facilities		✓
• Salaries/Benefits—Participant Time		✓
• Operating Expenses		✓
Ongoing Operations Cost (if applicable)		✓
Evaluation		✓
Overhead	✓	

Can you provide a copy of your cost guidelines? ☐Yes ☐No

13. An intangible is defined as a measure that is not converted to money because the conversion would be too expensive, not credible, or both. Here's a list of typical intangible benefits for a variety of programs.

Typical Intangible Benefits	
• Adaptability	• Employee complaints
• Awards	• Engagement
• Brand awareness	• Execution
• Career minded	• Image
• Caring	• Innovation
• Collaboration	• Job satisfaction
• Communication	• Leadership
• Commitment	• Networking
• Conflicts	• Organizational climate
• Cooperation	• Organizational commitment
• Corporate social responsibility	• Partnering
• Creativity	• Reputation
• Culture	• Resilience
• Customer complaints	• Stress
• Customer response time	• Talent
• Customer satisfaction	• Teamwork
• Decisiveness	

What is your approach to connecting intangibles to the program?

_____

_____

_____

14. When programs are evaluated at the application, impact, or ROI levels, the results must be communicated to the various audiences. Here's a list of possible combinations. Put a check mark by those that you have used to communicate results.

Communication Approaches				
Meetings	**Detailed Reports**	**Brief Reports**	**Electronic Reporting**	**Mass Publications**
Executives	Impact study	Executive summary	Website	Announcements
Management	Case study (internal)	Slide overview	Email	Bulletins
Stakeholders	Case study (external)	One-page summary	Blog	Newsletters
Staff	Major articles	Brochure	Video	Brief articles

Can you provide details on your communication guidelines? ☐Yes ☐No

15. What is the payoff of measurement and evaluation? Here are the possibilities. Please check all that apply.

ROI Methodology: The Payoff

_____ • Aligns projects to business needs

_____ • Shows contributions of selected projects

_____ • Earns respect of senior management/administrators

_____ • Builds staff morale

_____ • Justifies/defends budgets

_____ • Improves support for projects

_____ • Enhances design and implementation processes

_____ • Identifies inefficient projects that need to be redesigned or eliminated

_____ • Identifies successful projects that can be implemented in other areas

_____ • Earns a "seat at the table"

Can you provide any documentation that supports this issue? ☐Yes ☐No

16. How are measurement and evaluation data actually used? Below is a list of potential uses of evaluation data. Please indicate the extent of your use of evaluation data by circling all that apply by the specific level of data.

Use of Evaluation Data	Appropriate Level of Data				
	1	2	3	4	5
Adjust program design	✓	✓	✓		
Improve program delivery	✓	✓	✓		
Influence application and impact			✓	✓	
Enhance reinforcement			✓		
Improve management support			✓	✓	✓
Improve stakeholder satisfaction			✓	✓	✓
Recognize and reward participants		✓	✓	✓	
Justify or enhance budget				✓	✓
Develop norms and standards	✓	✓	✓		
Reduce costs		✓	✓	✓	✓
Market future programs	✓		✓	✓	✓
Expand implementation to other areas			✓	✓	✓

Can you provide documentation on the use of evaluation data? ☐Yes ☐No

17. Below are the best practices for conducting impact and ROI studies. Please indicate the extent to which you are following the best practices with a check mark.

ROI Methodology: The Payoff

_____ 1 The ROI Methodology is implemented as a process improvement tool and not as a performance evaluation tool for the staff.

_____ 2 ROI impact studies are conducted very selectively, usually involving 5 to 10 percent of projects and programs.

_____ 3 A variety of data collection methods are used in ROI analysis.

_____ 4 For a specific ROI evaluation, the effects of the program are isolated from other influences.

_____ 5 Business impact data are converted to monetary values.

_____ 6 ROI evaluation targets are developed, showing the percent of programs evaluated at each level.

_____ 7 The ROI Methodology generates a micro-level scorecard.

_____ 8 ROI Methodology data are being integrated to create a macro scorecard for the learning and development function.

_____ 9 The ROI Methodology is being implemented for about 3 to 5 percent of the budget.

_____ 10 ROI forecasting is being implemented routinely.

_____ 11 The ROI Methodology is used as a tool to strengthen/improve the programs and processes.

Can you provide documentation on your best practices? ☐Yes ☐No

Thank you for your input.

Follow-Up Survey
NSW Community Services

Purpose
The purpose of this survey was to follow up on use of skills from a caseworker development program for a cohort of Aboriginal staff in an Australian government agency.

Objectives
The following objectives serve as the basis for this survey:
1. Determine participant post-program reaction.
2. Determine usefulness of modules to participants.
3. Identify additional knowledge and skill gaps.

Source
O'Toole, S., and A. Dawood, (2012). Building and Managing an Effective Indigenous Workforce. In *Measuring ROI in Learning and Development: Case Studies From Global Organizations*, eds. P.P. Phillips and J.J. Phillips. Alexandria, VA: ASTD Press.

Table 8-3.

Aboriginal Staff Survey
Caseworker Training & Career Development
June 2006

PART ONE: About You

Providing the following information about yourself is voluntary. All information you provide on this survey will remain anonymous and is confidential.

This section is for all staff to complete.

Your Age: **Your Gender:** SELECT   **Your Region:**

How long have you worked for DoCS?   **Your Postcode:**

Is there anything else you think we should know about you?

PART TWO: Caseworker Development Course

If you have completed the CDC training in the last two years, please answer the following questions. If not please go directly to Part Three.

Thinking about the training you received in the Caseworker Development Course (CDC), please answer the following questions by selecting your answer from the drop down menu. If you have further comments, please provide them in the space below each statement. The more information you provide, the more improvements we can make.

1. **Has attending CDC training helped you to do your job?** SELECT

2. **Was the training delivered at a suitable level for you?** SELECT

3. **Were there things that made learning difficult for you?** SELECT
   If YES, what were they?

4. **Were there things that made learning easier for you?** SELECT
   If YES, what were they?

5. **Are there things that could have happened before the training started that might have made** SELECT
   completing the course easier?
   If YES, what are your suggestions?

6. **Have you been able to complete all of the assessment tasks?** SELECT

7. **Do you think that the assessment tasks equipped you to do your job?** SELECT

8. **Were there things that would have made the assessment tasks easier to complete?** SELECT
   If YES, what are they?

9. **Which of these modules has been the *MOST* useful to you?**

☐ Introduction to CDC	☐ Alcohol and Other Drugs	☐ Cultural Awareness
☐ Legal Responsibilities	☐ Responding to Domestic Violence	☐ Case Management
☐ Dual Diagnosis	☐ Mental Health	☐ Child Protection Dynamics
☐ Legal Issues	☐ Out of Home Care	☐ KIDS Training
☐ Working with Aboriginal Children & Families	☐ Affidavit Writing & Recording Evidence	☐ Interviewing Children and Gathering Evidence
☐ Conducting Secondary Assessments	☐ Building Relationships with Children, Young People & Careers	☐ Working with Children and Young People

Please provide comments:

10. **Which of these modules has been the *LEAST* useful to you?**

☐ Introduction to CDC	☐ Alcohol and Other Drugs	☐ Cultural Awareness
☐ Legal Responsibilities	☐ Responding to Domestic Violence	☐ Case Management
☐ Dual Diagnosis	☐ Mental Health	☐ Child Protection Dynamics
☐ Legal Issues	☐ Out of Home Care	☐ KIDS Training
☐ Working with Aboriginal Children & Families	☐ Affidavit Writing & Recording Evidence	☐ Interviewing Children and Gathering Evidence
☐ Conducting Secondary Assessments	☐ Building Relationships with Children, Young People & Careers	☐ Working with Children and Young People

Please provide comments:

Aboriginal Staff Survey: Caseworker Training & Career Development June 2006
Page 1 of 2

Aboriginal Staff Survey
Caseworker Training & Career Development
June 2006

11. How has CDC training assisted you in your work environment?

PART THREE: Career Development
Thinking about your job and your current skills and qualifications, please tell us about any further training, aspirations, and/or development you would like.

12. Are there any additional skills or knowledge you feel you need to do your job?   SELECT

   If YES, please provide further details below:

What is the skill/knowledge you would like to learn?	Why would you like to learn it?	What training or development do you need to be able to develop/learn this skill?	What are you current skills, qualifications, and/or experience in this area?
1.			
2.			
3.			
4.			

Please provide comments:

13. What do you find hard in your job?

14. What has been good in your job?

15. What type of support would help you to do your job?

16. Would you be interested in participating in a mentoring program?   SELECT

17. The ASB and L&D currently provide opportunities to enroll in the Diploma of Community   SELECT
Services (Protective Interventions). Would you be interested in enrolling in this course to be
completed on the job?

Thank you for your participation!

Your time and effort is greatly appreciated, and your answers will help us to develop a better, more useful online HR resource for all DoCS staff. You should now **SAVE** this document and forward it as an email attachment to **leanne.boyd@community.nsw.gov.au** in the **Aboriginal Services Branch.**

Semi-Structured Interview
U.S. Department of Defense

Purpose

This study represented a mixed method research approach to determine the strategic alignment of succession planning actions associated with efforts to build (versus buy) replacement workforce. This sequential explanatory research design included a quantitative survey as well as the interview questions provided here.

Objectives

The study set out to answer four research questions:

RQ1: How do military organizations ensure alignment of leadership and management development with strategic plans for investments in civilian workforce skill development?

RQ2: How do military organizations determine when to develop new civilian skills internally (make) or recruit new civilian workforce skills externally (buy)?

RQ3: As the Baby Boomers begin to retire, how do military organizations ensure hiring managers capitalize on strategic investments in civilian workforce skill development?

RQ4: How do military organizations use new leadership and management skills developed through investments in civilian workforce skill development?

Source

Jeffries, R.A. (2011). *Investments in Leadership and Management Succession Planning at a Department of Defense Organization in the Southeastern United States: A Review of Strategic Implications.* Doctoral dissertation. Human Capital Development: The University of Southern Mississippi.

Table 8-4. Succession Planning Interviews

Questionnaire for Supervisor and Hiring Managers

Please address the following questions and concerns concerning the leadership and management training program at the DODSE.

IQ1. One of the strategic goals of the DODSE is to invest in workforce training with regard to leadership and management skills. As a supervisor of graduates and non-graduates of the PH and Associates courses, how are the strategic implications of the leadership and management training communicated to the workforce?

IQ2. Why do you think there is a difference in perception between those who have taken the PH and Associates courses and other DODSE employees?

IQ3. Given the investment in leadership and management training at the DODSE since 2007, how should completion of the leadership and management training be used as a best-qualified criterion in hiring, promotion, or assignment of individuals to leadership positions within the DODSE?

IQ4. How are the graduates of the PH and Associates courses being used to fill the leadership and management skill gaps occurring due to the departure of managers?

IQ5. As a supervisor of graduates from the PH and Associates courses, how are you ensuring opportunities to apply the graduates' new skills gained during the training?

Annual Employee Survey
U.S. Department of Defense

Purpose

This study represented a mixed method research approach to determine the strategic alignment of succession planning actions associated with efforts to build (versus buy) replacement workforce. This sequential explanatory research design included a quantitative survey as well as the interview questions. The quantitative survey was a modified version of the U.S. Department of Defense Annual Employee Survey shown here.

Objectives

The study set out to answer four research questions:

RQ1: How do military organizations ensure alignment of leadership and management development with strategic plans for investments in civilian workforce skill development?

RQ1: How do military organizations determine when to develop new civilian skills internally (make) or recruit new civilian workforce skills externally (buy)?

RQ1: As the Baby Boomers begin to retire, how do military organizations ensure hiring managers capitalize on strategic investments in civilian workforce skill development?

RQ1: How do military organizations use new leadership and management skills developed through investments in civilian workforce skill development?

Source

Jeffries, R.A. (2011). *Investments in Leadership and Management Succession Planning at a Department of Defense Organization in the Southeastern United States: A Review of Strategic Implications.* Doctoral dissertation. Human Capital Development: The University of Southern Mississippi.

Table 8-5. U.S. DOD Employee Survey

U.S. Office of Personnel Management Annual Employee Survey:

In the National Defense Authorization Act for Fiscal Year 2004 (Public Law 108-136, November 24, 2003, 117 STAT. 1641), Congress established a requirement for agencies to conduct an annual survey of their employees to assess employee satisfaction as well as leadership and management practices that contribute to agency performance.

The results of this survey will assess:
- leadership and management practices that contribute to agency performance
- employee satisfaction with:
  - ▶ leadership policies and practices
  - ▶ work environment
  - ▶ rewards and recognition for professional accomplishment and personal contributions to achieving organizational mission
  - ▶ opportunity for professional development and growth
  - ▶ opportunity to contribute to achieving organizational mission.

The results from this survey will guide management in improving policies and programs designed to govern leadership and management practices, and improve overall employee job satisfaction.

2. DIRECTIONS: Please rate your overall job satisfaction level on the items listed below. Select the level that best represents your level of overall job satisfaction for each item below.

Employee Survey Questions Section I.	Strongly Agree	Agree	Neither Agree or Disagree	Disagree	Strongly Disagree	
Experiences: Personal/Work						
1. The people I work with cooperate to get the job done.						
2. I am given a real opportunity to improve my skills in my organization.						
3. My work gives me a feeling of personal accomplishment.						
4. I like the kind of work I do.						
5. I have trust and confidence in my supervisor.						
	Very Good	Good	Fair	Poor	Very Poor	
6. Overall, how good a job do you feel is being done by your immediate supervisor/team leader?						

Employee Survey Questions Section II.	Strongly Agree	Agree	Neither Agree or Disagree	Disagree	Strongly Disagree	Do Not Know
Recruitment, Development, & Retention						
7. The workforce has the job-relevant knowledge and skills necessary to accomplish organizational goals.						
8. My work unit is able to recruit people with the right skills.						
9. I know how my work relates to the agency's goals and priorities.						
10. The work I do is important.						
11. Physical conditions (for example, noise level, temperature, lighting, cleanliness in the workplace) allow employees to perform their jobs well.						
12. Supervisors/team leaders in my work unit support employee development.						
13. My talents are used well in the workplace.						
14. My training needs are assessed.						

Employee Survey Questions Section III.	Strongly Agree	Agree	Neither Agree or Disagree	Disagree	Strongly Disagree	Do Not Know
Performance Culture						
15. Promotions in my work unit are based on merit.						
16. In my work unit, steps are taken to deal with a poor performer who cannot or will not improve.						
17. Creativity and innovation are rewarded.						
18. In my most recent performance appraisal, I understood what I had to do to be rated at different performance levels (e.g., fully successful, outstanding).						
19. In my work unit, differences in performance are recognized in a meaningful way.						
20. Pay raises depend on how well employees perform their jobs.						
21. My performance appraisal is a fair reflection of my performance.						
22. Discussions with my supervisor/ team leader about my performance are worthwhile.						
23. Managers/supervisors/team leaders work well with employees of different backgrounds.						
24. My supervisor supports my need to balance work and family issues.						

Employee Survey Questions Section IV.	Strongly Agree	Agree	Neither Agree or Disagree	Disagree	Strongly Disagree	Do Not Know
Leadership						
25. I have a high level of respect for my organization's senior leaders.						
26. In my organization, leaders generate high levels of motivation and commitment in the workforce.						
27. Managers review and evaluate the organization's progress toward meeting its goals and objectives.						
28. Employees are protected from health and safety hazards on the job.						
29. Employees have a feeling of personal empowerment with respect to work processes.						
30. My workload is reasonable.						
31. Managers communicate the goals and priorities of the organization.						
32. My organization has prepared employees for potential security threats.						

Employee Survey Questions Section V.	Very Satisfied	Satisfied	Neither Satisfied nor Dissatisfied	Dissatisfied	Very Dissatisfied	Do Not Know
Job Satisfaction						
33. How satisfied are you with the information you receive from management on what's going on in your organization?						
34. How satisfied are you with your involvement in decisions that affect your work?						
35. How satisfied are you with your opportunity to get a better job in your organization?						
36. How satisfied are you with the recognition you receive for doing a good job?						
37. How satisfied are you with the policies and practices of your senior leaders?						
38. How satisfied are you with the training you receive for your present job?						
39. Considering everything, how satisfied are you with your job?						
40. Considering everything, how satisfied are you with your pay?						

Employee Survey Questions Section VI.	Strongly Agree	Agree	Neither Agree nor Disagree	Disagree	Strongly Disagree	Do Not Know
Command Specific/Strategic Alignment						
41. I am aware that a significant portion of the workforce at the DODSE will retire in the next 10 years.						
42. I am aware that the purpose of the leadership and management training program at the DODSE is to upgrade skills of current managers and replace skills lost as the aging workforce retires.						
43. I am aware that the replacement workforce will require different knowledge, skills, abilities, and behaviors than the retiring workforce.						
44. I am concerned about the aging workforce and the potential effects on the DODSE.						
45. The DODSE leadership communicates concern about the potential effects of the aging workforce.						
46. The DODSE is doing a good job assessing the potential impact of the aging workforce.						
47. The DODSE is preparing the workforce for potential leadership and management shortfalls created by the aging workforce.						
48. The DODSE has a viable strategy to replace the retiring Baby Boomer workforce.						

Employee Survey Questions Section VII.	Non-Supervisor	Team Leader	Supervisor	Manager	Executive	
Demographics						
What is your supervisory status?						
I have completed *both* of the following PH Associates courses (Chuck Sampson): Project Management *AND* Basic Supervisory Skills.	Yes	No				
Are you:	Male	Female				
Are you Hispanic or Latino?	Yes	No				
Please select the racial category or categories with which you most closely identify (Please select one or more):	White	Black or African American	Native Hawaiian or Other Pacific Islander	Asian	American Indian or Alaska Native	

Note: This survey is a standard OPM Annual Employee Survey administered to determine an organization's alignments with U.S. Office of Personnel Management human capital goals. Questions 41 through 48 are command-specific questions. Questions 44 through 48 are adapted from a workforce opinion survey used in Fedorek (2009).

Follow-Up Questionnaire
International Car Rental Company

Purpose

The purpose of this survey was to gather follow-up evaluation data on a leadership development program offered at a large car rental company based in the United States.

Objectives

The following program objectives served as the basis for the survey questions:

1. Participants will complete course requirements.
2. Participants will rate the program as relevant to their jobs.
3. Participants will rate the program as important to their jobs.
4. Participants will indicate opportunities for improving the course.
5. Participants must demonstrate acceptable performance on each major competency.
6. Participants will routinely use the competencies with team members.
7. Participants will report barriers and enablers to successful application of leadership competencies.
8. Participants and team members will drive improvements in at least two business measures due to the course, resulting in profit, cost savings, or cost avoidance.
9. Participants will identify additional benefits as a result of the program.

Source

Phillips, P.P., and J.J. Phillips. (2010). Global Car Rental. In *Proving the Value of HR: ROI Case Studies*, 2nd Edition, eds. P.P. Phillips and J.J. Philips. Birmingham: ROI Institute, Inc.

Table 8-6. Follow-Up Questionnaire

Program Name_____   End Date of Program_____

Our records indicate that you participated in the above program. Your participation in this follow-up survey is important to the continuous improvement of the program. Completion of this survey may take 45 to 60 minutes. Thank you in advance for your input.

CURRENCY

1. This survey requires some information to be completed in monetary value. Please indicate the currency you will use to complete the questions requiring monetary value. _____

PROGRAM COMPLETION

2. Did you O complete O partially complete O not complete the program? If you did not complete it, go to the final question.

REACTION

		Agree				Disagree
		5	4	3	2	1
3.	I recommended the program to others.	O	O	O	O	O
4.	The program was a worthwhile investment for my organization.	O	O	O	O	O
5.	The program was a good use of my time.	O	O	O	O	O
6.	The program was relevant to my work.	O	O	O	O	O
7.	The program was important to my work.	O	O	O	O	O
8.	The program provided me with new information.	O	O	O	O	O

LEARNING

		Agree				Disagree
		5	4	3	2	1
9.	The program was important to my work.	O	O	O	O	O
10.	I am confident in my ability to apply the knowledge/skills learned from this program.	O	O	O	O	O

11. Rate your level of improvement in skill or knowledge derived from the program content. A 0% is no improvement and a 100% is significant improvement. Check only one.

0%	10%	20%	30%	40%	50%	60%	70%	80%	90%	100%
O	O	O	O	O	O	O	O	O	O	O

APPLICATION

		Agree				Disagree
		5	4	3	2	1
12.	I routinely apply the knowledge/skills learned during the program.	O	O	O	O	O

		Frequently				Infrequently
		5	4	3	2	1
13.	How frequently did you apply the knowledge/skills learned during the program?	O	O	O	O	O

		High				Low
		5	**4**	**3**	**2**	**1**
14.	What is your level of effectiveness with the knowledge/skills learned during the program?	O	O	O	O	O
15.	Rate the effectiveness of the coach.	O	O	O	O	O

		Critical			Not Critical	
		5	**4**	**3**	**2**	**1**
16.	How critical is applying the content of this program to your job success?	O	O	O	O	O

		Very Well			Not Well	
		5	**4**	**3**	**2**	**1**
17.	To what extent did you stay on schedule with your planned actions?	O	O	O	O	O

18. What percent of your total work time did you spend on tasks that require the knowledge/skills presented in this program? Check only one.

0%	10%	20%	30%	40%	50%	60%	70%	80%	90%	100%
O	O	O	O	O	O	O	O	O	O	O

BARRIERS/ENABLERS TO APPLICATION

19. Which of the following deterred or prevented you from applying the knowledge/skills learned in the program? (Check all that apply.)

   ☐ no opportunity to use the skills
   ☐ lack of management support
   ☐ lack of support from colleagues and peers
   ☐ insufficient knowledge and understanding
   ☐ lack of confidence to apply knowledge/skills
   ☐ systems and processes within organization will not support application of knowledge/skills
   ☐ other

20. If you selected "other" above, please describe here.

   _____

21. Which of the following supported you in applying knowledge/skills learned in the program? (Check all that apply.)

   ☐ opportunity to use the skills
   ☐ management support
   ☐ support from colleagues and peers
   ☐ sufficient knowledge and understanding
   ☐ confidence to apply knowledge/skills
   ☐ systems and processes within organization will support application of knowledge/skills
   ☐ other

22. If you selected "other" above, please describe here.

   _____

RESULTS – 1st Measure

23. Please define the first measure you selected and its unit for measurement. For example, if you selected "sales," your unit of measure may be "1 closed sale."

   _____

24. For this measure, what is the monetary value of improvement for one unit of this measure? For example, the value of a closed sale is sales value times the profit margin ($10,000 x 20%=$2,000). Although this step is difficult, please make every effort to estimate the value of a unit. Put the value in the currency you selected, round to the nearest whole value, enter numbers only (e.g., $2,000.50 should be input as $2,000).

_____

25. Please state your basis for the value of the unit of improvement you indicated above. In the closed sale example, a standard value, profit margin, is used, so "standard value" is entered here.

_____

26. For the measure listed as most directly linked to the program, how much has this measure improved in performance? If not readily available, please estimate. If you selected "sales," show the actual increase in sales (e.g., 4 closed sales per month, input the number 4 here).You can input a number with up to 1 decimal point. Indicate the frequency base for the measure. _____

☐ daily   ☐ weekly   ☐ monthly   ☐ quarterly

RESULTS – 1st Measure

27. What is the annual value of improvement in the measure you selected above? Multiply the increase (question 26) by the frequency (question 26) times the unit of value (question 24). For example, if you selected "sales," multiply the sales increase by the frequency to arrive at the annum value (e.g., 4 sales per month x 12 x 2,000=$96,000). Although this step is difficult, please make every effort to estimate the value. Put the value in the currency you selected, round to nearest whole value, enter numbers only (e.g., $96,000.50 should be input as 96,000).

_____

28. List the other factors that could have influenced these results.

_____

29. Recognizing that the other factors could have influenced this annual value of improvement, please estimate the percent of improvement that is attributable (i.e. isolated) to the program. Express as a percentage out of 100%. For example, if only 60% of the sales increase is attributable to the program, enter 60 here. _____%

30. What confidence do you place in the estimates you have provided in the questions above? A 0% is no confidence, a 100% is certainty. Round to nearest whole value, and enter a number only (e.g., 37.5% should be entered as 38). _____%

RESULTS – 2nd Measure

31. Please define the second measure you selected and its unit for measurement. For example, if you selected "sales," your unit of measure may be "1 closed sale."

_____

32. For this measure, what is the monetary value of improvement for one unit of this measure? For example, the value of a closed sale is sales value times the profit margin ($10,000 x 20%=$2,000). Although this step is difficult, please make every effort to estimate the value of a unit. Put the value in the currency you selected, round to nearest whole value, and enter numbers only (e.g., $2,000.50 should be input as $2,000).

_____

33. Please state your basis for the value of the unit of improvement you indicated above. In the closed sale example, a standard value, profit margin, is used, so "standard value" is entered here.

_____

34. For the measure listed as most directly linked to the program, how much has this measure improved in performance? If not readily available, please estimate. If you selected "sales," show the actual increase in sales (e.g., 4 closed sales per month, input the number 4 here). You can input a number with up to 1 decimal point. Indicate the frequency base for the measure. _____

☐ daily   ☐ weekly   ☐ monthly   ☐ quarterly

35. What is the annual value of improvement in the measure you selected above? Multiply the increase (question 34) by the frequency (question 34) times the unit of value (question 32). For example, if you selected "sales," multiply the sales increase by the frequency to arrive at the annum value (e.g. 4 sales per month x 12 x 2,000=$96,000). Although this step is difficult, please make every effort to estimate the value. Put the value in the currency you selected, round to nearest whole value, and enter numbers only (e.g., $96,000.50 should be input as 96,000).

_____

36. List the other factors that could have influenced these results.

_____

37. Recognizing that the other factors could have influenced this annual value of improvement, please estimate the percent of improvement that is attributable (i.e. isolated) to the program. Express as a percentage out of 100%. For example, if only 60% of the sales increase is attributable to the program, enter 60 here. _____%

38. What confidence do you place in the estimates you have provided in the questions above? A 0% is no confidence; a 100% is certainty. Round to nearest whole value, and enter a number only (e.g., 37.5% should be entered as 38). _____%

39. What other benefits have been realized from this program?

_____

40. Please estimate your direct costs of travel and lodging for your participation in this program. Put the value in the currency you selected, round to nearest whole value, and enter numbers only (e.g., $10,000.49 should be input as $10,000).

_____

41. Please state your basis for the travel and lodging cost estimate above.

_____

FEEDBACK

How can we improve the training to make it more relevant to your job?

_____
_____
_____
_____

Thank you for taking the time to complete this survey!

Culture of Innovation Leadership Survey
Healthcare Organizations

Purpose

The purpose of the study was to determine the culture of innovation leadership competencies perceived by employees at high-performing and low-performing organizations. Leveraging the potential of an organization's workforce adds value to organizational processes, employee satisfaction, and customer loyalty.

Objectives

This survey set out to measure the following objectives:

RO1: Determine if there is a difference in a culture of innovation leadership between high readmission-rate hospitals and low readmission-rate hospitals.

RO2: Determine if there is a difference in problem-solving intelligence between high readmission-rate hospitals and low readmission-rate hospitals.

RO3: Determine if there is a difference in innovation management between high readmission-rate hospitals and low readmission-rate hospitals.

RO4: Determine if there is a difference in an organizational framework of innovation between high readmission-rate hospitals and low readmission-rate hospitals.

Source

Kirkby, C.Z. (2012). *Assessing a Culture of Innovation Leadership of the Human Capital in Healthcare.* Doctoral dissertation. Human Capital Development: The University of Southern Mississippi.

Table 8-7. Culture of Innovation Leadership Survey Instrument

Circle your level of agreement with one (1) being never, two (2) almost never, three (3) sometimes, four (4) often, and five (5) always.

Question	Never	Almost Never	Sometimes	Often	Always
1. My job description addresses how the role of innovative problem solving will benefit the organization.	1	2	3	4	5
2. My organization encourages innovative suggestions from employees.	1	2	3	4	5
3. I get timely feedback from my supervisor or leader on possible ideas I have developed for work-related problems.	1	2	3	4	5
4. When I have innovative ideas, my organization has a formal process available for me to submit the ideas.	1	2	3	4	5
5. I have taken a training class on innovative problem solving offered by my organization.	1	2	3	4	5
6. My organization has a formal process in place to seek ideas and innovative solutions from employees.	1	2	3	4	5
7. When faced with a work-related problem, I come up with multiple ideas.	1	2	3	4	5
8. My organization values the knowledge of employees by actively documenting each employee's unique skills. For example, CPR and the ability to speak multiple languages.	1	2	3	4	5
9. My supervisor or leader gives me timely feedback on possible ideas I have developed for work-related problems.	1	2	3	4	5
10. When working as a group, the team asks for input from everyone to solve work-related problems.	1	2	3	4	5
11. When solving work-related problems my supervisor listens to my input.	1	2	3	4	5
12. New knowledge and skills I develop on the job are actively documented by my organization.	1	2	3	4	5
13. The success of my organization depends on innovative thinking from employees.	1	2	3	4	5

14.	I come up with multiple ideas when faced with a work-related problem.	1	2	3	4	5
15.	The team asks for input from everyone when working as a group to solve work-related problems.	1	2	3	4	5
16.	When I determine how my innovative solutions will function within our organization, I present the solution to my supervisor(s).	1	2	3	4	5
17.	My organization has developed a formal process for employees to submit innovative ideas.	1	2	3	4	5
18.	My organization supplies employees with a formal problem-solving process to support innovation.	1	2	3	4	5
19.	My immediate supervisor encourages me to use innovative processes within my job function at work.	1	2	3	4	5
20.	To develop better solutions in the organization, my department works as a team.	1	2	3	4	5
21.	By actively documenting each employee's unique skills like certifications and bilingual, my organization values the knowledge of employees. For example, CPR and the ability to speak multiple languages.	1	2	3	4	5
22.	Having employees who are innovative thinkers plays a vital role in the success of my organization.	1	2	3	4	5
23.	To seek ideas and innovative solutions from employees, my organization has a formal process in place.	1	2	3	4	5
24.	My supervisor listens to my input on solving work-related problems.	1	2	3	4	5
25.	Training on the process of creative idea generation is provided to employees in my organization.	1	2	3	4	5
26.	The role of innovative problem solving and how it will benefit the organization is addressed in my job description.	1	2	3	4	5
27.	I am encouraged to use innovative processes within my job function at work by my immediate supervisor.	1	2	3	4	5
28.	In my organization, I have taken a training class on innovative problem solving.	1	2	3	4	5
29.	I consider all aspects of how the idea will impact the organization or customer when I come up with potential solutions to work-related problems.	1	2	3	4	5

30.	I present to my supervisor(s) how my innovative solutions will function within our organization.	1	2	3	4	5
31.	A formal problem-solving process supporting innovation is supplied by my organization.	1	2	3	4	5
32.	My department works as a team to develop better solutions in the organization.	1	2	3	4	5
33.	When I come up with potential solutions to work-related problems, I consider all aspects of how the idea will impact the organization or customer.	1	2	3	4	5
34.	My organization trains employees on the process of creative idea generation.	1	2	3	4	5
35.	My organization actively documents new knowledge and skills I develop on the job.	1	2	3	4	5
36.	Innovative problem solving is encouraged from employees in my organization.	1	2	3	4	5

9

Summary and Next Steps

 What's Inside This Chapter

This chapter gives a summary of important considerations for developing and administering your survey and analyzing and reporting your results. Upon completion of this chapter you should be able to:

▶ Describe the basics of an effective survey
▶ Develop objectives for your survey
▶ Design your research and survey questions
▶ Describe multiple administration techniques
▶ Use techniques to increase response rate
▶ Summarize and report data
▶ Develop an action plan to move forward
  with your survey project

The Basics

Use of surveys has grown tremendously in the learning and development field. This is mostly due to increased demand to show results of programs and projects and an increased interest in research data. Surveys are one of the most useful and popular techniques of collecting information from people to describe, compare, explain, or predict their knowledge, attitudes, or behaviors on various topics. Surveys are often used to gather data to isolate the effects of a program on improvement in business measures. They can also be used to influence or persuade an audience, make changes, or understand or predict behaviors or conditions. Data collected from surveys are often used to compare specific activities against activities of others.

Survey data can provide tremendous value to an organization. The value lies in the information obtained and the insight it can provide to executives. Surveys can uncover or forecast costs associated with making the wrong decision, and can reduce or uncover uncertainties related to those decisions.

Although surveys are valuable, like any data collection method, there is always some level of error. Error can be minimized by developing the survey instrument and administration plan carefully and concurrently. Types of potential errors include coverage errors, sampling errors, non-response errors, and measurement errors (Dillman, 2009). To keep instances of error low and develop the most effective survey instrument, you must employ:

- ▶ measurable objectives
- ▶ sound research design
- ▶ effective question design
- ▶ sound sampling strategy, when needed
- ▶ effective response strategy
- ▶ meaningful data summary
- ▶ effective data display and reporting.

It has been said that survey design and administration is a balance between art and science. Artistic and creative methods of asking questions, encouraging responses, and presenting results must be used to ensure your survey is effective. A more scientific approach is used to ask the right questions, avoid error, and administer the survey in an appropriate way for your organization. Adding to the balance is ethics. Here are a few basic ethical standards to follow:

- ▶ Take fiduciary responsibility of resources, rather than placing it on the client.
- ▶ Do not publish survey results without permission.
- ▶ Remember, the survey and subsequent results are the property of the client.
- ▶ Never impose bias in order to get certain results, even if requested by the client.
- ▶ Do not impose your own bias just to satisfy the client.
- ▶ Keep identities confidential and anonymous if promised at the onset of the survey project.
- ▶ To the best of your ability, never allow the client to use results to reprimand respondents.
- ▶ Use the appropriate type of analysis.

Survey Objectives

Like program objectives, survey objectives set the stage for an effective survey research project. Survey objectives are the basis for the survey questions, and are the result of a stated need. They define the kind of information that is needed for the most appropriate survey instrument, research design, source of data, and timing for data collection. By developing clear, measurable survey objectives early in the process, you subsequently increase the quality, value, and quantity of the data you receive. Objectives are critical and are paramount for survey design.

Developing clear objectives is the first step in designing the survey. Next comes writing questions, but before you start you must identify the specific information needs for each objective. Each objective includes one or more variables. Variables are entities that can take on different values and can be quantitative, qualitative, binary, composite, or even indirect measures.

Survey Research Design

Research design is an important component of the survey project. Research design specifies the groups to whom the survey will be administered and the timing of administration, to ensure the most useful and robust results.

The two designs to consider when constructing your survey are experimental design and descriptive design. When using experimental design, the researcher inserts an intervention of some sort and observes the outcome. With descriptive designs, the intervention or treatment has already occurred and associations rather than causal relationships are examined.

An important part of survey research design is sampling. Sampling is simply surveying the appropriate audience credibly so that inference can be made to a larger population. Sampling is an important and useful tool for many survey projects, but is not appropriate or necessary for all projects. As discussed in chapter 3, multiple techniques and online tools are available for selecting your sample.

Survey Questions

One of the most important considerations in survey design is designing good questions for your survey. The best survey questions are born from clear objectives that reflect specific measures. As you write your survey questions, try to read the respondents' point of view. Can they really answer your questions? Do they understand them? Have they had the appropriate information to be able to answer them? Are they willing to answer these questions? If not, you may need to consider rewriting or replacing your questions.

Once you have determined the appropriate questions to ask, you must choose the scale from which respondents will indicate answers. Many examples of scales, and which questions and settings are most appropriate for each, can be found in chapter 4.

Survey Instrument Design

Like the design of your survey questions, the design of your survey instrument plays an important role in ensuring your survey gathers the most relevant and useful information, in the quantities you need. Popular options for the layout of surveys include vertical, horizontal, and grid. In addition to the layout of the questions, the aesthetic qualities of your survey are also important. The font, spacing, and consistency of your survey can often influence the results. Like all components of your survey, consistency is key. Don't overuse bold or underlining and provide enough space between questions to eliminate the possibility of accidentally providing the wrong answer to the wrong question. The layout and design of your questionnaire should be carefully planned with logical and rational sequencing. When designing your survey, begin with the end in mind. That is, design your survey instrument for ease in tabulation and analysis and use technology when available.

When designing your survey instrument, additional correspondence and communication should be planned in order to ensure the highest response rate possible.

Participants should know about the survey in advance, as they are more likely to provide data and think about their responses if they are not blindsided by it. Even with plenty of notice, respondents are not always concerned with providing data quickly. A note or memo with the survey, or friendly follow-up reminders can help gather the most responses. When communicating about your survey, be sure to always include clear instructions and a point of contact, should the respondent have questions.

A final step in designing your survey is ensuring its validity and reliability. To be an effective data collection instrument, the survey should provide consistent results over time (reliability) and measure what it is intended to measure (validity).

Response Rates

Achieving the highest possible response rate is key to ensure the credibility of your data. The more responses you have, the more useable data you have for your calculation. For the highest response rate, advance, concurrent, and follow-up communication are important. In addition to the communication, consider the design of your survey as a tool for increasing response rates. Professional and simplistic surveys that respondents can move easily through typically yield higher response rates than clumsy or complicated surveys.

In addition to providing the best instrument, sometimes it is also helpful to show "what is in it" for the individual respondent. Using tangible and intangible rewards can serve as a motivator for respondents. Providing incentives and positioning respondents as the experts who can provide valuable information can also help increase response rates.

Data Summary and Reporting

Now that you've designed and administered your survey and collected the responses, it is time to analyze the results. Chapter 7 describes many methods for analysis of data such as descriptive statistics and basic statistical tests. After the data have been analyzed, you must be prepared to share them with the appropriate audience. There are two fundamental issues when it comes to developing your report: 1) the report outline and narrative and 2) graphical display of data. The key issue is to make your data interesting and compelling.

Sample Surveys

There are a variety of types of surveys and they are used for any number of purposes. Chapter 8 presents seven different surveys to demonstrate the different uses. Also, it is sometimes helpful when constructing a new survey, to review previously used questions. If you use any of the surveys offered in this chapter, we hope you'll respect the work of those who provided them and cite them as a source. But more important, we hope you find them helpful in demonstrating the basics of survey design.

Final Thoughts

The use of surveys will continue to grow. Rarely can you take a course, make a purchase, or even visit a website without being asked to rate your experience. Employers are more interested than ever in the productivity of their workforce and will continue to administer surveys to gather data from employees and consumers. Hopefully, by reading this book you have some basic questions and challenges to bring forth as you work with your team to develop surveys. We also hope you will use this information to critique surveys that come your way.

Getting It Done

Now that you know the basics of surveys, reassess your knowledge. Using the Survey Knowledge Scorecard shown in Table 9-1, rate yourself in terms of how much you know about the concepts listed. The scale is a 0-to-5 scale with 0 meaning you know nothing about the content area; and 5 meaning you know all there is to know. If you score 0 on any of the questions, revisit the corresponding section of the book. There are 20 content areas, so the highest possible score you can receive is 100 points. Compare your score with the score of the assessment you completed after chapter 1.

Once you have assessed your survey knowledge, complete the action plan shown in Table 9-2 to continue to develop and implement useful surveys and gather the heartiest data. To continue the conversation about survey design and administration, visit the ASTD Evaluation/ROI blog.

Table 9-1. Survey Knowledge Scorecard

For each content area, score yourself 0–5. Zero (0) means you know nothing about the content area. Five (5) means you know all there is to know. Note your ratings on each item and your total score. Once you have your post-reading score, develop an action plan to improve.

I know nothing	0	1	2	3	4	5	I know it all

Content Area	Score (0-5)
1. Types of surveys	
2. Types of error found in surveys	
3. Ethical considerations when administering surveys	
4. Types of survey objectives	
5. How to write SMART objectives	
6. Experimental research designs	
7. Descriptive research designs	
8. Writing quality survey questions (the stem)	
9. Writing quality response choices (the scale)	
10. Different types of survey scales	
11. Types of sampling procedures	
12. How to calculate sample size	
13. When to calculate sample size	
14. Techniques to ensure high response	
15. Descriptive statistics	
16. Measures of central tendency	
17. Importance of measuring variance	
18. Standard values like coefficient of variation and z-score	
19. Writing up the final report	
20. Graphical displays of data	
Total Score	

Highest possible score: 100 points   **Your previous score:** _____ points   **Your score now:** _____ points

243

Table 9-2. Action Plan for Developing Surveys

Name _____ Date_____ Evaluation Period _____ to _____

Objective_____

Action Steps	Expected Consequences	Target Date	Responsibility
1.			
2.			
3.			
4.			
5.			
6.			
7.			
8.			

Comments:

Appendix A

Answers to *Think About This* Exercises

■ ■

Below are the answers to the TAT exercises for which readers were asked to develop an actual response.

Chapter 3

Page 54: Federal Information Agency

Below is the comparison of turnover between the two groups:

Annualized Avoidable Turnover	1 Year Prior to Program	1st Year Sept. to Aug.	2nd Year Sept. to Aug.	3rd Year Sept. to Aug.	1 Year Post-Program
Total Group (1,500)	38%	39%	36%	35%	34%
Program Participants Group (100)	N/A	5% (5)	4% (4)	3% (3)	3% (3)
Similar Group (100)	N/A	34%	35%	33%	36%
Four-Year Expected Turnover Statistics = 138					
Four-Year Actual Turnover Statistics = 15					
Four-Year Total Group Turnover Statistics = 144 (with a base of 100)					

As you can see in the table, there is a significant difference in turnover between the two groups.

Question to Think About:

Of the eight threats to internal validity identified by Campbell and Stanley, which one threat is most obvious in this case study?

Correct answer:

Experimental Mortality/Attrition.

The turnover was so high in the agency that before the results of the study were complete, the entire control group left the organization. While the evaluation team kept replenishing the control group with comparative data, eventually, there was no match between the two groups.

While there is clear evidence just by the numbers that turnover for those in the program was much less than for those who were not in the program, the internal validity of the results was weak. So, it was decided to provide a more valid result of the connection between the program and the reduction in turnover, participants and managers provided insight into the percent turnover reduction actually attributed to the program. This estimate was adjusted for error.

Senior leaders accepted the results as credible.

Page 66: Sample Size Matching Exercise

Match each scenario below with the appropriate sample size technique.

A. Census

B. Simple Random Sample

C. Stratified Random Sample

D. Systematic Random Sample

E. Simple Cluster Sample

F. Convenience Sampling

Scenario	Sampling Technique
1. Sample is sorted by key variables before the sample is selected.	C
2. Every person in the organization has equal chance of being chosen.	B
3. Interviewing the entire group of participants.	A
4. Sampling populations at places where they can be easily reached.	F
5. Every seventh person on a list of eligible people is selected.	D
6. Groups are clustered by natural selection such as work location.	E

Page 70: Calculate the Sample Size

Solve for N_s.

Assume:

- $N_p = 800$

- $p = .5$

- $B = .03$ (+/− 3 percentage points)

- $C = 1.96$

What is the required sample size given the population, the proportion of the population to choose a response, the acceptable margin of error, and the z-score?

$N_s = $ _____

The correct answer is:

$$N_s = \frac{(800)(.5)(1-.5)}{(800-1)(.03/1.96)^2 + (.5)(1-.5)}$$

$$N_s = \frac{200}{(799)(.000234) + .25}$$

$$N_s = \frac{200}{.436966}$$

$$N_s = 458$$

Chapter 4

Page 86: Is It "Yes" or "No"?

Question to Think About

How could Marie have asked the question so that Patti would have opportunity to provide an accurate measure of her level of satisfaction?

Correct Answer

It's really hard to say if she could have done anything other than present the question in terms of a scale that included enough variance in response choice to give someone like Patti an option. This is an example of where the survey question is forcing the respondent to commit one way or the other. The follow-up questions provide opportunity for the respondent to express what was good or not so good about the service.

The point here is that the purpose of the survey and the specific survey objectives are the keys to successful survey questions. J.D. Power knows why they are trying to force a Yes or No response—it's just that Marie didn't know what exactly to do with Patti.

Chapter 7

Page 160: Calculate the Measure of Central Tendency

Measure of Central Tendency	Data	Answer
Mode	15, 20, 21, 20, 36, 15, 25, 15	15
Median	15, 20, 21, 20, 36, 15, 25, 15	20
Mean	15, 20, 21, 20, 36, 15, 25, 15	20.88

Page 166: Describe the Data

The table below is the output generated through Minitab, a statistical software package. The output describes the measures of central tendency and dispersion for the data from the above example. What can you say about the data?

N	Mean	StDev	Variance	Minimum	Median	Maximum	Range	Mode
8	20.88	7.08	50.13	15.00	20.00	36.00	21.00	15

Answer: The average (mean) of the eight scores is 20.88 ranging from 15 to 36. The most frequently selected response is 15. The standard deviation of 7.08 indicates the spread of the data. If there were a "normal" distribution of data, the standard deviation would tell you that 95% of the scores fall between 6.72 and 35.04.

References and Resources

■■

Alreck, P.L., and R.B. Settle. (2003). *The Survey Research Handbook*, 3rd edition. New York: McGraw Hill.

Alreck, P.L., and R.B. Settle. (1995). *The Survey Research Handbook*, 2nd edition. New York: McGraw Hill.

Armstrong, W.W. (1974). *Dependency Structures of Data Base Relationships*, page 580-583. IFIP Congress.

Bartrum, D. (2003). Testing Through the Internet, in *Encyclopedia of Psychological Assessment* (R. Fernandez-Ballesteros, ed.) p. 985. London: Sage.

Blankenship, M. (June 11, 2009). Do Cell Phones Affect Telephone Surveys. Public Opinion Research Blog. *Mark Blankenship Enterprises*, http://publicopinionresearch. blogspot.com/2009/06/do-cell-phones-affect-telephone-surveys.html (accessed June 6, 2011).

Broderick, M. (2009). "On the Road to ROI: A Current Report on How Audience Response Systems Deliver Value in Corporate Training Applications," http://www.turningtechnologies.com/media/files/Turning%20Technologies%20ARS%20ROI%20 Whitepaper.pdf (accessed July 8, 2011).

Campbell, D.T., and J.C. Stanley. (1966). *Experimental and Quasi-Experimental Designs for Research*. Chicago: Rand McNally.

Carifio, J., and R. Perla. (2007). Ten Common Misunderstandings, Misconceptions, Persistent Myths and Urban Legends About Likert Scales and Likert Response Formats and Their Antidotes. *Journal of Social Sciences, 2*, 106-116.

Cialdini, R.B., N. Eisenberg, B.L. Green, K. Rhoads, and R. Baton. (1998). Undermining the undermining effect of reward on sustained interest: When unnecessary conditions are sufficient. *Journal of Applied Social Psychology, 28*: 249-63.

Cook, L.S., J.L. White, G.C. Stuart, and A.M. Magliocco. (August 13, 2003). "The reliability of telephone interviews compared with in-person interviews using memory aids." *Annals of Epidemiology, 13*(7).

Dillman, D.A., J.D. Smyth, and L.M. Christian. (2009). *Internet, Mail, and Mixed-Mode Surveys: The Tailored Design Method*, 3rd edition. Hoboken: John Wiley & Sons, Inc.

Few, S. (2012). *Show Me the Numbers: Designing Tables and Graphs to Enlighten*. Oakland: Analytics Press.

Fink, A. (2003a). The Survey Handbook, 2nd edition. In Fink, A. (editor) *The Survey Kit, Volume 1*. Thousand Oaks: Sage Publications.

-------. (2003b). How to Design Survey Studies. In Fink, A. (editor) *The Survey Kit, Volume 6*. Thousand Oaks: Sage Publications.

-------. (2003). How to Sample in Surveys, 2nd edition. In Fink, A. (editor) *The Survey Kit, Volume 7*. Thousand Oaks: Sage Publications.

Flynn, F.J. (2003). What have you done for me lately? Temporal adjustments to favor evaluations. *Organizational Behavior and Human Decision Processes,* 91: 38-50.

Fowler, F. J. (1995). *Improving Survey Questions*. In Applied Social Research Methods Series Volume 38. Thousand Oaks: Sage Publications.

Garner, R. (2005). Post-It Note Persuasion: A sticky influence. *Journal of Consumer Psychology,* 15:230-37.

Glass, Peckham, and Sanders (1972). Consequences of failure to meet assumptions underlying the analyses of variance and covariance, *Review of Educational Research,* 42: 237-288.

Goldstein, N.J., S.J. Martin, R.B. Cialdini. (2008). *Yes! 50 Scientifically Proven Ways to Be Persuasive*. New York: Free Press.

Harter, J.K., F.L. Schmidt, E.A. Killham, and J.W. Asplund. (2006). Q^{12} Meta-Analysis. Gallup, Inc., http://strengths.gallup.com/private/Resources/Q12Meta-Analysis_Flyer_GEN_08%2008_BP.pdf (accessed May 12, 2012).

Horowitz, H. (1988). *Student response systems: Interactivity in a classroom environment,* http://www4.uwm.edu/ltc/srs/faculty/docs/HorowitzIBMSRS.pdf (accessed July 8, 2011).

Irvine, A., P. Drew, and R. Sainsbury. (2010). Mode effects in qualitative interviews: a comparison of semi-structured face-to-face and telephone interviews using conversation analysis. *Research Works, 2010-03,* Sociology Policy Research Unit: University of New York.

Isaac, S., and W.B. Michael. (1971). *Handbook in Research and Evaluation*. San Diego: EdITS.

Jamieson, S. (2004). Likert scales: How to (ab)use them. *Medical Education,* 38: 1212-1218.

Kirkpatrick, D.L. (1998). *Evaluating Training Programs*. San Francisco: Berrett-Koehler.

Kleeman, J., E. Shepherd, and J. Phaup. (2010). *Embedded Assessments: Building Knowledge Checks, Surveys and Other Assessments into Learning Materials*. Norwalk, CT: Questionmark Corporation, http://www.questionmark.com/us/whitepapers/index.aspx (accessed June 1, 2011).

Kusek, J.A., and R.C. Rist. (2004). *Ten Steps to a Results-Based Monitoring and Evaluation System*. The World Bank.

Lubke, G.H., and B.O. Muthen. (2004). Applying Multigroup Confirmatory Factor Models for Continuous Outcomes to Likert Scale Data Complicates Meaningful Group Comparisons. *Structural Equation Modeling*, 11: 514-534.

Maddux, W.W., E. Mullen, and A.D. Galinsky. (2008). Chameleons bake bigger pies and take bigger pieces: Strategic behavioral mimicry facilitates negotiation outcomes. *Journal of Experimental Social Psychology*, 44: 461-68.

Maio, G.R., J.M. Olson, L. Allen, and M.M. Bernard. (2001). Addressing discrepancies between values and behavior: The motivating effect of reasons. *Journal of Experimental Social Psychology*, 37: 104-17.

Marrelli, A.F. (2010). Conducting Interviews. In Phillips, P. P. (editor) *ASTD Handbook of Measuring and Evaluating Training*. Alexandria, VA: ASTD Press, pp. 85-95

McMurray, D.P. (2001). TRAINING/Presentations. Scantron Corporation.

Meltzoff, J. (1998). *Critical Thinking About Research: Psychology and Related Fields*. Washington, D.C.: American Psychological Association.

Ott, R. L., and M. Longnecker. (2010). *An Introduction to Statistical Methods and Data Analysis*, 6th edition. Belmont, CA: Cengage Learning.

Phillips, J.J. (1983). *Handbook of Training Evaluation and Measurement Methods*. Houston: Gulf Publishing.

Phillips, J.J., and L. Edwards. (2009). *Managing Talent Retention: An ROI Approach*. San Francisco: Pfeiffer.

Phillips, J.J., and P.P. Phillips. (2010a). *Measuring for Success: What CEOs Really Think About Learning Investments*. Alexandria, VA: ASTD Press.

Phillips, P.P., and J.J. Phillips. (2010b). Measuring ROI in Interactive Selling Skills. In *Proving the Value of HR ROI Case Studies*, 2nd edition. Birmingham: ROI Institute, Inc., pp. 139-155.

Phillips, J.J., and P.P. Phillips. (2008). *Beyond Learning Objectives: Develop Measurable Objectives that Link to the Bottom Line*. Alexandria, VA: ASTD Press.

Phillips, P.P., and C.A. Stawarski (2008). *Data Collection: Planning for and Collecting All Types of Data*. San Francisco: Pfeiffer.

Raghubir, P. (2004). Free gift with purchase: Promoting or discounting the brand? *Journal of Consumer Psychology*, 14: 181-86.

Schrock, S.A. and W.C. Coscarelli. (2007). *Criterion-Referenced Test Development: Technical and Legal Guidelines for Corporate Training*, 3rd edition. San Francisco, CA: Pfeiffer.

Smith, K. (2010). *Selecting Technology to Support Evaluation*. In the *ASTD Handbook of Measuring and Evaluating Training* (Chapter 22). Alexandria, VA: ASTD Press.

Starr, G.J., D.E. Dal Grande, A.W. Taylor, and D.H. Wilson. (October 23, 1999). Reliability of self-reported behavioral health risk factors in a South Australian telephone survey. *Australian and New Zealand Journal of Public Health, 5,* pp. 528-30.

Stevens, S.S. (1946). On the Theory of Scales of Measurement. *Science. 103*(2684): 677-680.

Surowiecki, J. (2005). *The Wisdom of Crowds.* New York: Doubleday.

Swanson, R.A., and E.F. Holton III, eds, (2005). Chapter 6 - Experimental and Quasi-experimental Designs. *Research in Organizations: Foundations and Methods of Inquiry.* San Francisco: Berrett-Koehler.

Tufte, E.R. (2001). *The Visual Display of Quantitative Information,* 2nd edition. Cheshire, CT: Graphics Press.

The Gallup Management Group, http://gmj.gallup.com/content/20311/Work-Feeling-Good-Matters.aspx#1.

Trochim, W.M. (2006). The Research Methods Knowledge Base, 2nd Edition. Internet WWW page, http://www.socialresearchmethods.net/kb/ (version current as of October 20, 2006).

Uebersax, J.S. (2006). Likert scales: Dispelling the confusion. *Statistical Methods for Rater Agreement* website, http://john-uebersax.com/stat/likert.htm (accessed: December 2, 2012).

Additional Resources

■■

The following are just a few of the resources available to help you design and administer effective surveys.

Associations/Organizations

American Association for Public Opinion Research

www.aapor.org

American Evaluation Association (AEA)

www.eval.org

American Statistical Organization (ASO)

www.amstat.org

Association of Academic Research Organizations (AASRO)

www.aasro.org

Council of American Research Organizations (CASRO)

www.casro.org

European Survey Research Association

www.europeansurveyresearch.org

For a complete list of academic and nonprofit Survey Research Organizations, visit: http://www.srl.uic.edu/lansro.htm, retrieved September 11, 2012.

Books

Cochran, W.G. (1977). *Sampling Techniques*, 3rd edition. San Francisco: John Wiley.

Fink, A. (2002). *The Survey Kit*, 2nd edition. Thousand Oaks: Sage Publications.

Harris, R.L. (1999). *Information Graphics: A Comprehensive Illustrated Reference*. Oxford: Oxford University Press.

Hart, C. (1999). *Doing a Literature Review: Releasing the Social Science Research Imagination.* Thousand Oaks: Sage Publications.

Kalton, G. (1983). *Introduction to Survey Sampling.* Thousand Oaks: Sage Publications.

Kish, L. (1995). *Survey Sampling.* San Francisco: Wiley-Interscience.

Machi, L.A. and B.T. McEvoy. (2011). *The Literature Review: Six Steps to Success.* Thousand Oaks: Corwin Press.

Rumsey, D.J. (2011). *Statistics for Dummies.* San Francisco: John Wiley.

Salkind, N.J. (2010). *Statistics for People Who (Think They) Hate Statistics,* 4th edition. Thousand Oaks: Sage Publications.

Salkind, N.J. (2011). A Study Guide for: *Statistics for People Who (Think They) Hate Statistics,* 4th edition. Thousand Oaks: Sage Publications.

Yau, N. (2011). *Visualize This: The FlowingData Guide to Design, Visualization, and Statistics.* San Francisco: John Wiley.

Technology & Software

Atlas.ti

   www.atlasti.com

Dedoose

   www.dedoose.com

HyperResearch

   www.researchware.com

IBM SPSS

   www-01.ibm.com/software/analytics/spss/

KnowledgeAdvisors

   www.knowledgeadvisors.com

Minitab

   www.minitab.com

NVivo

   www.qsrinternational.com

Poll Everywhere

   www.polleverywhere.com

Qualtrics

   www.qualtrics.com

QuestionPro

   www.questionpro.com

RaoSoft

   www.raosoft.com

SAP
>   www.sap.com

SAS
>   www.sas.com

SurveyMonkey
>   www.surveymonkey.com

SurveyPro
>   www.apian.com

Tableau Software
>   www.tableausoftware.com

Websites

American Evaluation Association: Qualitative Software Resources
>   www.eval.org/Resources/QDA.asp

Likert Scale Options
>   Siegle, D. Neag School of Education, University of Connecticut
>   www.gifted.uconn.edu/siegle/research/instrument%20reliability%20and%20validity/
>   likert.html

Methodspace: Home of Research Methods Community
>   www.methodspace.com

Random Numbers Generator
>   GraphPad
>   www.graphpad.com

ROI Institute, Inc.
>   www.roiinstitue.net

Sample Size Calculator
>   www.raosoft.com/samplesize.html

Social Research Methods Knowledge Base
>   www.socialresearchmethods.net

Survey Research Laboratory
>   University of Illinois at Chicago
>   www.srl.uic.edu

Index

About the ROI Institute

■■■

ABOUT THE ROI INSTITUTE

The ROI Institute, Inc. is the leading resource on research, training, and networking for practitioners of the Phillips ROI Methodology.

With a combined 50 years of experience in measuring and evaluating training, human resources, technology, and quality programs and initiatives, founders and owners Jack J. Phillips, PhD, and Patti P. Phillips, PhD, are the leading experts in return on investment (ROI).

The ROI Institute, founded in 1992, is a service-driven organization that strives to assist professionals in improving their programs and processes through the use of the ROI Methodology. Developed by Jack Phillips, this methodology is a critical tool for measuring and evaluating programs in 18 different applications in more than 60 countries.

The ROI Institute offers a variety of consulting services, learning opportunities, and publications. In addition, it conducts internal research activities for the organization, other enterprises, public sector entities, industries, and interest groups. Together with their team, Jack and Patti Phillips serve private and public sector organizations globally.

BUILD CAPABILITY IN THE ROI METHODOLOGY

The ROI Institute offers a variety of workshops to help you build capability in the ROI Methodology. Among the many workshops offered through the ROI Institute are:

- One-day *Bottomline on ROI* Workshop—provides the perfect introduction to all levels of measurement, including the most sophisticated level, ROI. Learn the key principles of the ROI Methodology and determine whether your organization is ready to implement the process.
- Two-day *ROI Competency Building* Workshop—the standard ROI Workshop on measurement and evaluation, this two-day program involves discussion of the ROI Methodology process, including data collection, isolation methods, data conversion, and more.

ROI CERTIFICATION™

The ROI Institute is the only organization offering certification in the ROI Methodology. Through the ROI Certification process, you can build expertise in implementing ROI evaluation and sustaining the measurement and evaluation process in your organization. Receive personalized coaching while conducting an impact study. When competencies in the ROI Methodology have been demonstrated, certification is awarded. There is not another process that provides access to the same level of expertise as the ROI Institute's ROI Certification. To date, over 5,000 individuals have participated in this process.

For more information on these and other workshops, learning opportunities, consulting, and research, please visit us on the web at **www.roiinstitute.net,** or call us at **205.678.8101.**

About the Authors

■■

Patti Phillips, PhD

Patti Phillips, PhD, is president and CEO of the ROI Institute, Inc., the leading source of ROI competency building, implementation support, networking, and research. A renowned expert in measurement and evaluation, she helps organizations implement the ROI Methodology in 40 countries around the world. Since 1997, following a 13-year career in the electric utility industry, Phillips has embraced the ROI Methodology by committing herself to ongoing research and practice. To this end, she has implemented ROI in private sector and public sector organizations. She has conducted ROI impact studies on programs such as leadership development, sales, new-hire orientation, human performance improvement, K-12 educator development, and educators' National Board Certification mentoring. Her current work includes research and application of the ROI Methodology in workforce development, community development, and social sector programs.

Phillips teaches others to implement the ROI Methodology through the ROI Certification process, as a facilitator for ASTD's ROI and Measuring and Evaluating Learning Workshops, and as adjunct professor for graduate-level evaluation courses. She serves on numerous doctoral dissertation committees, assisting students as they develop their own research on measurement, evaluation, and ROI. Patti serves as faculty at the UN System Staff College in Turin, Italy; she also serves as Principal Research Fellow for The Conference Board.

Phillips's academic accomplishments include a PhD in international development and a master's degree in public and private management. She is a certified in ROI evaluation and has been awarded the designations of Certified Professional in Learning and Performance and Certified Performance Technologist. She contributes to a variety and journals has authored a number of books on the subject of accountability and ROI, recent titles include: *Measuring the Success of Coaching* (ASTD Press, 2012); *10 Steps to Successful Business Alignment* (ASTD Press, 2012); *The Bottomline on ROI 2nd Edition* (HRDQ, 2012); *Measuring Leadership Development: Quantify your Program's Impact and ROI on Organizational Performance* (McGraw-Hill, 2012); *Measuring ROI in Learning and Development: Case Studies from Global Organizations* (ASTD Press , 2011); and *The Green Scorecard: Measuring the ROI in Sustainability Initiatives* (Nicholas Brealey, 2011). Patti Phillips can be reached at patti@roiinstitute.net.

Jack Phillips, PhD

Jack J. Phillips, PhD, is a world-renowned expert on accountability, measurement, and evaluation. Phillips provides consulting services for Fortune 500 companies and major global organizations. The author or editor of more than 75 books, he conducts workshops and presents at conferences throughout the world.

Phillips has received several awards for his books and work. On three occasions, Meeting News named him one of the 25 Most Powerful People in the Meetings and Events Industry, based on his work on ROI. The Society for Human Resource Management presented him an award for one of his books and honored a Phillips ROI study with its highest award for creativity. The American Society for Training & Development gave him its highest award, Distinguished Contribution to Workplace Learning and Development for his work on ROI. His work has been featured in the *Wall Street Journal, BusinessWeek*, and *Fortune* magazine. He has been interviewed by several television programs, including CNN. Phillips serves as President of the International Society for Performance Improvement.

His expertise in measurement and evaluation is based on more than 27 years of corporate experience in the aerospace, textile, metals, construction materials, and banking industries. Phillips has served as training and development manager at two Fortune 500 firms, as senior human resource officer at two firms, as president of a regional bank, and as management professor at a major state university. This background led Dr. Phillips to develop the ROI Methodology¾a revolutionary process that provides bottom-line figures and accountability for all types of learning, performance improvement, human resource, technology, and public policy programs. Phillips regularly consults with clients in manufacturing, service, and government organizations in 44 countries in North and South America, Europe, Africa, Australia, and Asia.

Phillips and his wife, Patti P. Phillips, PhD, have recently published books such as *Measuring the Success of Coaching* (ASTD Press, 2012); *Measuring Leadership Development: Quantify your Program's Impact and ROI on Organizational Performance* (McGraw-Hill, 2012); *10 Steps to Successful Business Alignment* (ASTD Press, 2011); *The Green Scorecard: Measuring the Return on Investment in Sustainability Initiatives* (Nicholas Brealey, 2011); *and Project Management ROI* (John Wiley, 2011).

Phillips has undergraduate degrees in electrical engineering, physics, and mathematics; a master's degree in decision sciences from Georgia State University; and a PhD in Human Resource Management from the University of Alabama. He has served on the boards of several private businesses—including two NASDAQ companies—and several nonprofits and associations, including the American Society for Training & Development and the National Management Association. He is chairman of the ROI Institute, Inc., and can be reached at jack@roiinstitute.net

Bruce Aaron, PhD

Bruce Aaron discovered the field of measurement and evaluation while working his way through graduate training in school psychology, when he took a part-time position as an evaluation consultant with the local school district.

His affinity for the work led him to a PhD in Educational Measurement and Evaluation. For several years, Bruce was responsible for the evaluation of major grant programs for the 8th largest school district in the U.S., and served as a consultant to the State of Florida on program evaluation and assessment design projects.

He joined Andersen Consulting, later Accenture, as an evaluation consultant and spent several years at the company where he served as an executive with global responsibility for evaluation of training and knowledge management programs. Bruce founded Ametrico in 2010 to continue to develop accountability concepts and services for organizations seeking solutions in evaluation, measurement, assessment, and certification.

With more than 20 years of program evaluation experience, Bruce has presented at international conferences of organizations such as ASTD, ISPI, SALT, AERA, FERA, EERA, AEA, and The Psychometric Society.

Bruce has authored or co-authored dozens of presentations, articles, chapters, and books, including *Isolation of Results: Defining the Impact of the Program* with Jack Phillips, and a chapter for *The ASTD Handbook of Measuring and Evaluating Training*.

Bruce received his MA in School Psychology and PhD in Educational Measurement and Evaluation from the University of South Florida, and is a Certified Professional in Learning and Performance (CPLP).